THE COU

The Courage Circle

How to Live in Truth and Dare

Sandy Stream

The Courage Circle.
By Sandy Stream

ISBN: <u>978-0-9938828-5-2</u>

Cover and Chapter Illustrations: CoverKitchen PTD.

Interior Illustration: Nathaly Osorio-Rios

Copyright © 2023 Sandy Stream Publishing.

Montreal, Canada.

thecouragecircle.com

Table of Contents

Opening Up

THE WORDS ON THESE PAGES reflect how I have managed to get through difficult times and to come out on the other side intact and free.

I decided to document my personal experiences in the hope that they might be of help to you, and to my children, in finding some clarity and peace while navigating this thing called Life.

At first, this book might seem "messy" with its intertwined sections. That is because life is messy, not linear. But eventually, these pages might just start to make sense to you—as they did for me. You might start to see the *order* and even the *beauty* of the chaos in action.

So, if you can, open yourself up just a little bit before immersing yourself into these pages, and know that you can always choose to take whatever helps you and set aside what does not.

I have absolute faith that your brilliant navigation system will guide you on how to best align with the stars.

Sandy Stream

Creating The Courage Circle

The Courage Circle

IF YOU THOUGHT THIS BOOK would teach you how to create a great big Circle of Courage with many people to feel safe and strong and to find your power, then let me clear this up from the very start.

The first circle that you will need to create is **around yourself.**

This circle is around you, where you start to look inward to see the Truth. The Truth is all you look for... and ironically, the Truth is so hard to see because it is often accompanied by pain.

But pain you must endure in order to see clearly, and to find your

COURAGE
TO
BE

This book is about Fear, Truth, and Honesty: words with many meanings.

And how am I, a lawyer with twenty years of experience teaching contract law to purchasing professionals, going to teach about the Truth, the whole Truth, and nothing but the Truth?

Here's the cool part: I don't have to teach it! Because if I just show it to you, then the Truth can speak for itself.

I believe we all have a "sixth sense" for the Truth and cannot hide from it forever. It's as though we have an inner lie detector.

We *feel it* in our bodies and a part of us *knows* when something is True. And once we have been exposed to a Truth, it's hard to fully escape it. It will keep gnawing at us until we acknowledge it.

So, if in this book I put a light on something, you will see it. But I will not try to convince you of it, or try to prove anything to you. I will simply point it out and it can speak for itself.

You will either look at it or look away, but this is not in my control.

Are You Actually Ready
for the Truth?

IT CAN BE DIFFICULT AND painful to see the Truth, but it can also be liberating. Once you are open to seeing painful Truths, then you are also open to freedom. They go hand in hand.

For example, if you face a painful Truth from your childhood (one of the most difficult Truths), you are opening the possibility of being freed from the lies and stories you might have created about it and then, perhaps, stopping the unhealthy coping mechanisms you have used to deal with it or deny it.

So, what if, instead of *fighting* or avoiding the Truth and the pain you feel, **you allow them to be**?

Well, at times, it might feel like you will die from the pain of it all. And actually, that is true in a way: Something will die (perhaps some of the stories you've created to deal with life), and it can be scary to have beliefs die. Those stories feel like a part of us, so it can be hard to let them go.

But what if I told you that on the other side of having your stories "killed" by Truth, there is peace? Would you be so afraid?

Here are some initial glimpses of Truths, as I see them, that you may not have considered. Some might be familiar to you and some might be new.

᪥

False: My feelings are all over the place. I must not be normal.
Truth: You have feelings, and it's a normal part of being human to have feelings. Period.

✧

False: I'm not good enough the way I am.
Truth: There is no evidence to support this. The existence of that *thought* is not proof and does not make it True. You were born for this life and, therefore, made perfectly.

By the way, this phrase "being good enough" still sounds negative to me, since it implies that if you did come to think you are "good enough," it would still be less than, or missing, something more that you could be. It implies you are settling for mediocre. So, I prefer to use the phrase, "You are goodness." The Truth is **you are goodness** inside. That sounds right!

✧

False: I'm helpless, and there's nothing I can do.
Truth: You are help*ful*—*full* of possibilities to make choices, to support and guide the situation to its possibilities, including the possibility of asking for help.

✧

False: I better develop thick skin.
Truth: If you have thick skin, you cannot connect with yourself or with others.

❧

False: I have to adjust myself so people don't reject me.
Truth: No, you don't.

❧

False: I have to change so many things.
Truth: You cannot change the present since it's already here.
You can only accept the present and make choices in that mo-
ment. There's a difference.

❧

False: I have to get to a certain "point" in life.
Truth: There are no points in time. Life is constantly flowing
and changing. You cannot stop this flow.

Now that I have pointed to some possible Truths, good luck trying to avoid them! Remember, your body knows and feels when
things sound true...

Deeply Perfect

LET'S START AT THE VERY beginning of you when you were miraculously brought into this life. You were born absolutely and completely perfect.

Now, I have written just one sentence above, and already your **self-doubt begins**—about your nature and about that "crazy" sentence I dared to write.

You are perfect in a
deep sense.

Every thought in your head likely disagrees with me. But that's what thoughts do: they are criticizers, analyzers, measurers, distrusters, controllers—basically, they are the **robot** in you.

Actually, I prefer to think of these kinds of thoughts as coming from "the Calculator." It calculates and measures everything all day long. Calculators are certainly useful on occasion... but I would not let a Calculator run my life!

For how could a Calculator understand my feelings, my passions, my deepest desires, my true nature? How could a Calculator measure love, peace, and freedom?

It can't. And this is why I do not entrust my life to this "thinking" part.

Instead, I've learned to look at my center, my body, my breath, and my heart for guidance. And this is what this book is about — finding the Courage to find the *real you*, the perfect *soul* or *essence* that you are, with its unique mission or path, and then to have the Courage to walk that path.

It is no easy feat to find the *true you* and follow your true path. What am I talking about?

What if I told you that if you look deep inside, without all the noise around you, then it's there?

YOU are there.
YOU have always been there.
YOU will always be there.

The only question is how skilled you have become at *hiding yourself* or pretending or avoiding.

I am not judging *why* you would hide your *true self*. I understand. After all, the whole world has been giving you millions of messages about why you should hide the *true you* and act and look a certain way instead.

And it can definitely be scary to be the *real you* in our current world! That's why we need Courage; to keep going when people around us might disapprove, criticize, or shun us.

Have you ever noticed that the word "encourage" has the word "Courage" in it? That's why encouraging each other can light a powerful spark! My wish is that at least one sentence in this book will light that spark for *you.*

Now, if you are feeling slightly open and ready to start exploring your *true* nature, or to continue if you've already begun, then the obvious question is, "How can I find it?"

Well, the path is complex and different for each of us. So, I'm going to write a bunch of pieces under seven chapters and hopefully, one or many of the pieces of this puzzle are part of yours.

As you start to read the following pages, try not to worry about the question, "What if I show my true self?" Instead, ask yourself "What if I *don't?*"

You deserve peace, and the only peace there is, as far as I have seen, is the peace of sitting in your own true nature.

We may not have met in person (yet), but I am one human being on this earth who firmly believes in you—the *real you*—and who wants to encourage you on this path of remembering.

Remembering who you are.

"What Is Wrong with Me?"

You have likely been living with these words in your head since you were a child... words that have been put there by *others*.

"You need to improve."

"You have a good side and a bad side."

"You are a sinner."

"You're not good enough."

"You need to perform certain actions to be valuable."

... "What is wrong with me?" you might think.

How painful it is to have so many people in our lives put us down, control us, judge us, reject us... How painful it is that our brains took in this information and believed it!

And thus, the "judge in our head" was created at some point when we were children so we could ensure that our parents or other caretakers didn't reject us completely. We adjusted to make ourselves "acceptable" and worth taking care of so that we might be fed and sheltered in order to survive. "Rebelling against" or "not believing" our own parents was not an option. But now that we are older, we can ask the question:

What if it's all not true?

What if you are actually "just right" on the inside? And what if you are simply going about life, learning, making mistakes, and just trying to find your path?

What if nothing is wrong with you at all?

What if all those overt or subtle put-downs were nonsense?

The Truth is powerful and can challenge and disbalance the ego, the Calculator thoughts.

The Truth can be found inside the body. And in this book, we will reclaim our bodies. We have been "de*corp*itated" (our bodies cut off and ignored while living in our Calculator heads), and that's why this Truth is elusive.

The Truth is already in your body, in your emotions, and in your heart. You simply have been ignoring, invalidating, or avoiding them all for a long, long time...

Your Innocence

I BELIEVE YOU ACTUALLY KNOW YOU are deeply innocent. But there is a big difference between *thinking* and *knowing*.

You might have a lot of awful *thoughts* about yourself. Perhaps you put yourself down, thinking you are not good enough in terms of your appearance, achievements, or discipline. Perhaps you are filled with guilt. **But if you look deeply into the body and the heart instead, this knowledge about your deep innocence and goodness exists**. You just haven't taken enough time to feel, understand, and have compassion for yourself.

Perhaps you have not sat with yourself in meditation or practiced self-awareness movements to get to know yourself deeply.

So, if you are ready to move away from asking, "What's wrong with me?" then it's time to look at a different question:

"What did I go through?"

It all likely started when you were young. When you felt sad or upset, did you speak to anyone who allowed your feelings without judging or "fixing" you? Were you allowed to be sad or mad? I'm not suggesting you should have thrown things or expressed your anger in ways that might be hurtful, but were you allowed to just *feel* mad about something? It's unlikely, from what I have seen. Thus the "decorpitation" began... **It became "illegal" to feel.**

Or what if, as a child, you wanted to sing and felt joy in singing, but people said you were "crazy" or "not good at it," so you rejected this piece of yourself? Your inner child is wise, an expert in the fun and lightness of being. Were you allowed to show and express your inner child and *feel* joy in singing or dancing? Or were you told that this is not okay or told not to spend time on that? Thus, the decorpitation continues, "adjusting" yourself to please others.

They were all telling you, "You're not allowed to feel," "Don't feel this," "Something is wrong with you," and, "Your body is wrong."

Don't believe them!

There is nothing to fix, and we waste a lot of energy trying to fix ourselves instead of *allowing* our feelings. We spend so much time rejecting and suppressing ourselves.

But this is all healable. It's not too late to **Come Out, Come Out, Wherever You Are!**

Nothing Is "Wrong"

MY FRIEND RECENTLY TEXTED ME, "What's wrong?" And although I had just separated from my husband, whom I love deeply, and was in heartache, and even though my son and daughter were also struggling, and even though we were all in the middle of Covid-19 difficulties, I just deeply *felt*:

Nothing is "wrong."

Nothing is wrong, and life cannot be "wrong."

This is where we have to start on the courageous road: with Trust. We have to trust something. Trust that life is on its course, that you are on your path or being directed to it if you just listen. There *is* a direction, although it can be so incredibly hard to see sometimes!

And here you are, at this very moment, reading these very words—**and your whole life has brought you here, right now.**

Why right now? Only you will know...

Things fit together in ways we sometimes cannot see in the moment. So just Trust that all your suffering has led you here and things are as they should be.

You may think this means that life does whatever it wants, that you have *no power, no choice.*

Quite the contrary!

Your **choice** and **power** are probably what you are looking for in reading this book, and I'm hoping you will better understand how to use these as you go through the next chapters.

Choice is what makes us human.

We choose all the time: to follow the rules, to speak, not to speak. The minute you think you "have to" is where you have learned **not to see your power.** You are so used to things that you don't realize you have a choice.

So maybe you don't have full Trust in life yet, and that's okay. But *a little bit* of Trust in life is a good start, and perhaps it will build in time as you open up to new Truths.

So, if you're ready to look inside and see what's going on, what's True, and what's Y♥U, then let's get started.

Finding "You"

Your Voice

INSTEAD OF GETTING ANALYTICAL USING your Calculator, let's start by choosing a song you like and then singing or humming it. You will need to do this over and over again by yourself and in your Courage group (if you choose to form a group at home after reading this book to discuss its contents and to do some suggested practices).

In singing, you are looking for your voice. You don't really need to *do anything* to find it. You just need to **STOP doing** certain things to hear it.

STOP trying to sound good.
STOP trying to improve.
STOP trying to impress anyone.
STOP comparing your voice to others.
STOP faking your voice.

Then you will hear your own voice.

This is where we start. In the shower, in the bath, in bed, wherever. Start to hear and use y♥ur natural voice.

In your Courage group, each person can choose to express their most authentic voice (even by just saying "hello" or their name) and notice if there is any judging of good or bad vs. *just listening*.

Keep circling until you are able to express a sound without judging it as good or bad. One step at a time. You (and everyone there) are learning how to be unapologetically you.

And isn't that ridiculous... that you would ever need to apologize for *being you*? Notice how often you say "I'm sorry" before or after you speak or act. What are you apologizing for?

I'm hoping something in these pages will encourage you to

be y♥urself
unapologetically.

Black Sheep

WE OFTEN WALK AROUND IN our daily life afraid to be different, scared to be left out, and obsessing about the possibility of being rejected. Others have led us to believe that we need to "fit in."

But is it even possible to be the real, unique you while walking around with these fears that cause you to fake your way through life?

If we are all unique and innately valuable—which is what I believe—then what are we supposed to "fit into" exactly? It makes no sense.

It's not an easy thing to say, "Don't worry about rejection, being left out, and being judged." Most parents at least partially "reject" their children in one way or another, as do our peers when we're children and adults. These are painful experiences, and so we learn to "adjust" ourselves so as not to be rejected!

But I'll tell you what's even more painful: Walking around for the rest of your life **rejecting yourself!**

Think about it: You are actually the only person who can truly approve or reject yourself.

When someone "rejects" you, they are sending a message that, "You are a bad apple," "defective," "not good enough," and so on.

But if someone rejects Y♥U, *the beautiful apple*, you do not have to accept this message as Truth. The apple is not "bad" because it wasn't taken or admired by someone *else*.

This is not a Truth!

It only means that the other person doesn't want or respect or understand this apple, for whatever reason *is in them*. That's why you are the only one who can actually reject yourself, as the apple you are, if you *internalize* their action and accept *their* thoughts.

So here is your first chance to take your power back. For years you've been giving the power to approve or disapprove of you to your parents, friends, colleagues—and even your children.

TAKE IT BACK!

You are now the only one who can reject or approve yourself. They are all powerless!

Now... with this power back in your hands, will you accept or reject yourself? That's a tough one. Our own Calculator loves to criticize.

Here is an exercise that might help, and one you can do anywhere, anytime. During this simple exercise, try to see your thoughts as an overworking Calculator and practice sending this overheated, electrical energy down to the ground and receive new energy in your **heart.** You can do this simple exercise whether sitting or standing.

Inhale for four seconds while closing your eyes and feel energy from your feet to your crown, as if you are sucking up water from the ground up to your head.

Pause for two seconds at the top of the breath (your crown).

Exhale for six to eight seconds and imagine your overheated Calculator(head) energy moving down to the earth.

With every breath, nourish yourself and receive new energy from the earth's core, and release thoughts down into the earth. Slowly start to listen for *deeper truths* in this space.

Do this at your own rhythm. As you inhale, slowly *open your heart space*. It's very important for you to practice at your own rhythm, since the synchronizing of the breath and heart is unique to each one of us.

This is the beginning of loosening the grip of the Calculator and reviving yourself. You are slowly learning to feel deeper parts of yourself instead of focusing on the Calculator thoughts.

No effort is required since you are already Y♥U.

Truly Unique: The Simple Truth

CAN YOU PUT ASIDE THINKING about people being "in" or "out," black sheep or white sheep, **or any other color or shape?**

I propose we live with a real understanding of uniqueness—recognizing the worth and perfect inner uniqueness of every single individual.

This does not mean we have to accept any kind of behavior. We are looking at the deeper level of *essence* and recognizing the inner being—even when that being is perhaps not seeing clearly right now, struggling to see their worth, or is wounded and perhaps acting out.

But before we worry or think about *other people* and why they do what they do... are you able to see *yourself* as an absolutely unique individual?

Unique: definition
being the only one of its kind; unlike
anyone or anything else.

The Point System

As we already saw, many of us walk around using the Calculator to compare, judge, and criticize. Here is a challenge I have for this "scientific" Calculator:

Challenge: Can you actually calculate and measure who is "better" than who and allot points on an Excel sheet?

What if I smiled at my neighbor today? Does that count? Do I get a point?

What if I painted for three years in my room to recover from grief and now can get back to living? What's my "worth"? Did I lose points for taking time to grieve?

What's my number if I'm tall?

Description	Points
Money	
Tall	
Kind gesture	
Got out of bed despite grief	
Smiled at the bus driver	
Cried	
Three university degrees	

This point system makes no sense. Release and let go of performance and measurement. We're human *beings*, not human *doings*. **Our innate value is simply in being.** We don't have to do anything to be "energetic souls," living in our "essence," "spirit," or whatever word you like to use.

Once this is accepted, each person can follow the path they are inspired to without judgment or comparison. And ironically, they might end up actually "doing" a lot! But that "doing" would be coming from the right place, not from the fears we have been talking about.

Everyone has a value of being here, whether you understand it today or not.

If you want to feel your true value and self-worth, then just sit on the floor. You do not have to do ANYTHING at all. Anyone who tells you otherwise is trying to control you or is misguided themselves.

It's very easy to control someone by telling them they aren't good *unless* they do this or that. It will keep you busy for hours, days, and years trying to "fix yourself" instead of **living your life**!

Pain

MANY OF US WALK AROUND avoiding painful feelings, but this can be a mistake. **Only through seeing the Truth and feeling our pain can we grow**.

If you refuse to see the Truth and feel old pain, then your body will always be under stress trying to show it to you through anxiety, malaise, dis-ease, and other messages.

It's as if there is an eclipse over your own heart. Instead, can you stop covering things up and Trust the wisdom of your body to deal with this hurt?

If you create a Courage group after reading this book, share a painful experience with someone and notice how the feeling passes after sitting with it, allowing it and crying if your body needs to. Grief and pain are part of life. If you refuse to live them as they come, then you cannot live in peace. They will get "stored" in your body until you let them out with tears, a painting, a scream—whatever.

What is your relationship with pain? Do you view feeling and acknowledging your pain as a weakness? Do you get annoyed when others feel pain? If pain is *truly there*, then why are you getting upset at it? It takes Courage to see the world as it is. To be in reality.

> "These pains you feel are messengers. Listen
> to them." – Rumi

What if the pain is a *message* to you on how to move along on your path? What if it is the teacher or guide of what you are to do next? Avoiding it decorpitates you, and so you will continue to walk around like a head without a body. **Re-engage your inner compass by feeling everything.**

Your compass is NOT in your head. It's in the body—and specifically in the heart.

Avoiding Feelings

I SAW A WOMAN FALL OFF her bike the other day, and she seemed to have major pain in her back. I rushed over and suggested she wait a moment and not rush to get up—but she absolutely didn't want to sit on the sidewalk. She seemed to be experiencing shame... the shame of falling and of feeling pain.

A few moments later, her friend pulled up, and she quickly stood up and got into the friend's car. Who knows what damage was done to her spine by rushing like this? I guess **being seen in a state of weakness and vulnerability** was too much for her to tolerate.

Instead of accepting help (she refused to lean on her own friend to walk over to the car), she seemed more concerned about how she was being "seen." I am not judging this. It was just sad for me to witness it.

We suffer when we *avoid* feeling our pain or believe there is *shame* for having it. If we remain in our head, we are avoiding feeling, and it "keeps us safe" in a way, at least for the moment, when it might be overwhelming. But when we consistently avoid feeling our sadness, hurt, fear, or any other feeling, the head gets busy creating stories instead of **feeling and processing all our emotions and letting them guide us.**

And if we avoid and refuse to feel "negative" emotions, then we are likely avoiding *all* feelings in general, leaving us chronically uneasy and anxious.

Once we learn to get past shame (which I will discuss later) and start *feeling*, we will likely experience some pain or perhaps a lot of pain. But we can eventually get past it and start experiencing moments of love, joy, and peace as well, in harmony with the cycles of life.

We get the whole human experience.

But to experience anything, we need a direct physical experience, to *feel* it, and this is why all help and self-help methods that focus on the *body* are helpful, whether it be dancing, shaking, massaging, hugging, crying, screaming, writing, painting, or meditating.

And this is why "talking" is often not the most useful practice unless it is with someone who *really* knows how to validate, accept, and give space for *all feelings* without judgment, in which case it can be extremely helpful (Thanks CaraLynne ♥). That person with whom you talk would need to be non-judgmental with their own feelings—but in my experience, *most people are not,* so choose wisely.

The habit of avoiding pain and feelings is often born in our families. Dysfunctional families don't acknowledge pain and hide it. In particular, "negative" feelings are not "allowed." They are ignored and dismissed, or we are told those feelings need quick "fixing." Everyone walks around pretending everything is okay **when actually, there is a lot of pain in these homes.**

This demonization of emotions seems to exist to some extent in many, if not most, homes. If you were not brought up in a home where *all* emotions were welcomed, then you will need to revisit and relearn to allow them. It's no easy feat.

Once you understand that there are no negative emotions, there are just emotions, which are **all welcome and true**, you are on your way... on a path that might take years to unravel, but you are on your way!

Starting to Feel

P<small>AIN HURTS, AND IT WILL</small> keep showing up, since what doesn't heal, repeats. *Feel the pain* because it is from the heart, and it will guide you!

Even sadness, anger, and pain are gifts towards our self-compassion and a compass for our choices. All our emotions are **guiding us** to a greater state of being.

As we know, a lot of people repress emotions, but you can choose to release control and start allowing them. You are the main repressor of your emotions. Of course, you can continue avoiding your feelings forever... or you can **choose** to start observing and feeling them.

We are just talking about *feeling*—not acting out or doing anything to anyone. Just sitting and *feeling everything*.

"The cure for the pain is the pain." – Rumi

A Painful Truth

ONE OF THE MOST PAINFUL truths many avoid is that they have been loved *conditionally*, whether by a parent or partner. This is a deep wound.

Unconditional love does not mean a partner staying with you, or a parent allowing any behaviors, or not having boundaries. It is a felt love about your essence, your possibilities and your goodness.

But when this doesn't happen—which, in my experience, is the case for most of us except a rare few who have actually experienced true unconditional love—it is *very* painful.

It pains our heart and it pains the Universe, because it is not aligned with reality and Truth. The Truth is that we are all **lovable unconditionally**. We are good, just fine and perfect the way we are, even if we make mistakes.

It is a deep pain, perhaps the deepest pain of all, if your parents did not love you unconditionally. This sad and difficult reality might take years, or even a lifetime, to recover from because it intentionally or unintentionally sends the message (which you might have internalized) that you are not lovable, are impure, or are somehow defective.

The interesting thing about this kind of love, however, is that (at least in current times) it is unlikely it can be experienced to its fullest extent from another anyway, even from parents.

It might very well be that the only "deep and unconditional love" you will truly experience is the one you will find in your own being by knowing, accepting, and understanding yourself completely, with full compassion.

You might also encounter one of the rare individuals in our world who actually feels *deep love for themselves and for everyone*; it's something you can see in their eyes and feel in their presence. These people make the world go around since they have the ability to "wake up" or "bring to light" this Truth in everyone they encounter.

Seeing another human who looks at you that way is a gift. And it can be quite healing if you have not yet realized who you are. But such people, *for now*, are very rare—until more people wake up to this Truth in themselves.

So, hold on to the Truth and understanding about yourself, no matter what the people around you feel towards you. Allowing every aspect of yourself *to be* is what healing is. Take all the parts of you that you put aside and start putting yourself back together.

Loving yourself **unconditionally** is something you can achieve in this lifetime. And that is the best thing ever!

> "Why are you knocking at every other door?
> Go, knock at the door of your own heart."
> — Rumi

Sitting with Pain

Wʜᴇɴ ʟᴇᴀɴɪɴɢ ɪɴᴛᴏ ᴏᴜʀ ᴘᴀɪɴ instead of avoiding it, sometimes we need support, so please learn to seek and ask for it, whether it be to find someone to listen to you, give you a hug, make a meal for you, or recommend resources to you. Slowly we can also realize that we have our own powerful internal ability to support the situation.

We have our "masculine energy" (which has nothing to do with gender, as I'll discuss later) in our spine to help hold and support us as we feel our feelings.

Our spine. Our strength. Our sword.

Sit straight on the floor or chair and feel your spine, and ask it to hold you together when you are falling apart.

While in pain, you can also try to locate where the pain is in your body. Where exactly do you feel the wound? It is often in the heart, and how sad this is. In a meditative state, you can give it *energy* (love, light, compassion; whatever works for you).

In the midst of your pain, questions might come to mind. But instead of asking, "Why is this happening to me?" try asking: "Why is this happening *for* me? What am I here to learn?"

Sit with the pain and get support as needed. Ask yourself if there is something this experience is telling you about what **you need to do next in your life**. You are learning to *feel*.

Sitting in meditation is not just about relaxing. It's about *feeling*, becoming more alive, and experiencing the spectrum of emotions. And listening to them.

Once you are sitting in Truth, your Truth, there is an indescribable strength that starts to build slowly but surely. Because this Truth I'm talking about is not actually *just yours*. It is about being aligned with Life when you are present in your body, accepting all reality... including your feelings.

You are not disassociating from Life anymore. You are with Truth and reality, and everything is "right," no matter how hard it might seem in the moment.

Truth and reality cannot be "wrong."

They just are.

Vulnerability

You MAY THINK IT IS not safe to be yourself. You may think that if you are yourself, you won't receive love.

This is an illusion.

The Truth is you likely won't get full love *from the outside* or full acceptance *from the outside*. (Again, unless you meet one of those extremely rare individuals who deeply loves and accepts *everyone* unconditionally.) So, if you look for love and acceptance on the *outside*, you will become dependent on getting a crumb here and there, and it will become your drug. You will not be "okay" unless someone loves you unconditionally... **and is that really possible for *most* people to offer right now?**

What is possible, however, is for you to do and feel this *yourself!* You have the ability inside. No matter what, and no matter who has abandoned you, **you do not have to abandon yourself!** No matter what someone else might say, do, or think. You *know* your Truth. You *know* your experience better than anyone in this world!

And what to do with this Truth you feel? Well, you open slowly and allow your Truth, whatever it is, **to be in the world**. You slowly open up and start to connect with others and with life at a deeper, more honest level.

In order to have a relationship with anyone, be it a friend, partner, or neighbor, you will need to be open and vulnerable. When we are completely closed to others, we are likely completely closed to ourselves. When we are guarded and have lots of walls up, we might be avoiding our Truth, intimacy, and vulnerability.

Of course, you can choose not to open to anyone and take no risks. But then you will likely have only superficial relationships, never know yourself deeply, and be lonely.

Unfortunately, many people, and in particular men, have been taught and shamed into avoiding all feelings. Their emotions were demonized, and so they were taught to hate and hide parts of themselves. They've been taught to **look down on anyone who shows their humanity.** They've been told:

"Don't cry."
"Be a man."
"Don't be a pussy."
"Don't be weak."

This has led many people to become "insensitive." They can no longer *sense* themselves deeply—let alone anyone else. They have been decorpitated from their bodies, where their feelings and deeper selves reside.

Feeling and sharing does not make men or women or anyone illogical or weak. It makes us honest, brave, and compassionate. It opens the world and allows us to feel intimately connected.

Opening to Others

WHEN OPENING, WE CAN DO so without abandoning ourselves and while still protecting our wellbeing.

Do not open to people who are dismissive, demeaning, cold, and "rejecting." Do not open to those who act as if they are superior, as they are not ready to relate with healthy respect and equality. They are also not ready to support and encourage you.

Their goal (intended consciously or not) is to put you down so as to feel better about life or about themselves. They live purely in their Calculator heads. This includes many in the helping professions, in my experience.

If someone says something unkind to you, you do not need to sit there and take it; you can speak up, or you can walk away and choose not to share with that person. But hopefully, you can take some risk and open up and be truthful with people who seem safe, so you can share your wounds and get support.

Consciously choose whom to open up to and whom not to. After some time, you will become a bit of an expert at trusting your inner guidance system. And you will know who is "safe," when to open up, and when to set and express your boundaries.

For example, if you meet a person who is closed down, then don't share with them. Or if they are partially open, and you share, but then they shame you, you can express yourself (that you feel hurt or upset), set a boundary, and make some choices about whether to keep interacting with them. You do not try to control them; you simply make a **choice** to keep opening up or spending time with them or not.

Here's another example: Do you keep sharing with a parent or partner who does nothing but dismiss you? Why do you keep sharing? Are you repeating the pattern hoping for a different outcome to heal your pain?

It won't work, and your parent or partner might never "get it." You might need to heal and deal with this pain differently... perhaps on your own, with a therapist, with movement practices, or otherwise.

We are all still growing and still somewhat partially vulnerable, and many of us are still wounded inside. We can protect ourselves so as not to become *more* wounded by being aware of our current state of fragility and taking care of ourselves *like a mother bear does her cubs.*

Accept and understand this fragility; do not criticize it. This is Truth—and *all Truth is allowed and accepted.* So, simply ask yourself what your fragile part or wound needs. Can you observe and listen to what is *actually* happening inside? Ask yourself the question:

"What do I need? And how can I meet this need?"

You'd be surprised at how many needs do not require another person to fulfill them. We have **a lot of resources inside of us!**

But, of course, another compassionate human can also be the magical softening that allows us to feel safe while processing any difficulties. Seek help when you are fragile. And when you are solid, offer your stability for others to lean on.

Most importantly, start to see how you are not a good listener, how you are not compassionate, how you hurt people with your judgments. What you are doing to others is surely a reflection of what you are doing to yourself.

The more of us there are in the world who know how to listen and be a safe space for others to share their Truth, the less "dangerous" it is for everyone to be open, to be themselves, and to be vulnerable.

Seeing Yourself as a Victim

Before i talk about the perils of being a "victim," I would like to talk about the opposite problem: When we *refuse* to "be the victim" and thereby **avoid seeing our pain**.

In my experience, many people have a belief that was ingrained in them that they should not feel sorry for themselves. This idea, played over and over, can actually be a hindrance to feeling your pain and having compassion for yourself.

Yes, you are allowed to feel your full suffering and to notice and understand how hard it was for you.

This is NOT feeling sorry for yourself!

This is NOT "being a victim."

It is self-compassion.

Acknowledging how much you have suffered might bring a deep sadness for what you went through, and **this is healthy and needs to be felt.**

Basically, it is a "grief for the self, a painful but liberating experience of compassion for the self."[1]

We need to move past the thoughts of, "I hate myself for being weak," or "I blame myself." Maybe imagine putting yourself on

---

[1] Hendel, Hilary Jacobs. *It's Not Always Depression*. Penguin Random House.

a chair and pretending it's someone else sitting there... Do you think that person should have been treated that way? If not, then you know what that person **deserved,** and you can turn that into **compassion for self.**

We need to understand what we went through, and we need to *feel for ourselves.* Cry for ourselves. Feel all the hurt of not being loved, accepted, cared for, seen, or heard by a parent, partner or others.

Doing so is scary sometimes. Once we are allowed to feel pain, we can sometimes get stuck deep in there and not see the way out. Here are some suggestions to move forward and to *not* get stuck:

1. Try to find one thing you did to actually contribute to this painful situation—how you participated in this somehow. For example, I recall feeling so upset that someone was completely absent when I had a medical emergency. I allowed myself to feel angry and hurt. But then I looked at how *I* participated in this situation and realized it was by having incorrect expectations of this relationship. I had felt let down in similar ways by them before and I kept thinking the next time would be different. From then on, I decided to act in accordance with reality instead of my old, incorrect view of the relationship.

    Another example was when I experienced feeling invalidated by someone. I looked for my part and saw that I had been "allowing it" for too long. This is NOT "blaming the victim." Understanding if and how you participated does not remove another person's responsibility for their actions. It can actually be empowering for you, as it removes the mental state of feeling total helplessness; that life just does what it does, and you can't do anything about it. Even if you find only *two percent participation* on your part, this will help you move forward.

2. Try to see what **choice** you have **NOW.**

This might be hard to see, especially if the mind is in a vicious circle or fixated on a hurt. But choosing to make a simple decision while the head is spinning, like, "I'm going to take one breath before I continue thinking about this," can break this fixation! **Choice is personal power.** You can, of course, use your power of choice to seek help and support.

Your Posture

TAKE A LOOK AT YOUR posture; ask someone to take a picture of it for you if you like. It will show you how you are *feeling*.

Does your posture change with different people? How so?

Don't try to fix this! Just look!

Just notice your posture with different people... Are you slumped, with your head down? Are you breathing easily or nervously? Are you feeling open? Your posture will guide you to know what you are feeling with that person and whether the relationship is healthy for you.

Or it can be a great indicator of your relationship with yourself.

Over time, you can practice holding your space on the planet, standing with a straight, tall, yet relaxed and flexible spine, no matter your actual height.

Stop trying to be invisible.

"No" = Self-Love

ONE DAY, AS I WAS waiting for my daughter to finish a class, I came upon a mother yelling at her daughter, who was about thirteen or fourteen years of age. The girl was sitting on a bench in some kind of prom dress, with her head down. Clearly, she was distraught.

The mother kept insulting her. "You are an idiot!" she said, along with many other putdowns.

I wasn't sure what to do. The mother's anger was high... and the girl's head was so low. Her posture was heartbreaking. So, I made a choice.

The mom walked away briefly as I was passing the girl on the bench, and I looked at her and softly whispered, "You are not an idiot."

I know that as children, it is hard to set and express boundaries, especially those involving our parents. So, it would have been very scary and difficult for this teenager to stand up to her mother. But as we get older, we can slowly learn to express our boundaries and move toward whatever feels right to us.

Saying "NO" = self-love

"No, I'm not an idiot."
"No, I'm not ugly."
"No, I can't do that; I'm resting tonight."
"No, you can't treat me or insult me like that."

"No, I am going to choose what I want to do: dye my hair; speak up; take that job."

When you say no when it is true to you, you build self-confidence slowly but surely.

There is a difference between an inflated ego and *self-confidence in who you truly are*. Healthy self-confidence is calm and relaxed. It's when you are self-assured and not trying to prove anything to anyone or be superior to anyone.

And if you are still dealing with an *inner critic*, realize that it is **not you** or **yours**. Who spoke to you that way in the past? Who put that critic in your head?

Question it
and stand up to it!

The more you do this, the better you get at it. Soon your **INNER PROTECTOR** will get stronger than your inner police or inner critic that keeps you in line, controlled, or fitting in. And you will start caring for yourself as a mother bear protects her cubs.

Perfectionism

ARE YOU TRYING TO BEHAVE in a certain way that will maximize approval from the outside? Perfectionism is unauthentic because you have rejected the *true self*.

Perfectionism is an attempt to be perfect from some *outside* standard. The irony is that it's caused by not seeing the Truth of the actual perfection that *already* exists on the inside!

Our inner perfection and inner nature do not need fixing.

Where a person dealing with Perfectionism might say: "This thing needs to be done perfectly, so it looks good and is 'right.'"

A person trusting in their Inner Perfection might feel: "I don't care about how this looks to others right now. I want to do something I care about, regardless of whether someone else approves of my choice. My inner nature calls me to do it, and I trust my inner voice to guide me."

Striving for outer-based perfection is a recipe for misery and powerlessness, since the **outside is fully controlling our behavior**, which will never measure up. And we are likely also expecting others in our circle to act a certain way so everything looks good to the outside world or is "perfect" in some way.

Instead, if a person knows their inner perfection, inner goodness, or unique essence, then *the whole act of self-measuring* is simply not present, and they can start to live a **self-directed life**.

Shame and Guilt

ATTEMPTING TO CONTROL SOMEONE ELSE'S feelings is one way that some people try to control others. They want someone else to feel this or that for any number of reasons, but often it's because it makes *them* feel better in some way.

Some people manipulate others by trying to induce **guilt** or **shame**. They might try to convince you something is "bad" or "wrong" about you so they can get you to do what *they* think you should do.

Unhealthy shame arises when you are living under the control of others, and *they* decide whether you are "good," "bad," "deserving," or "valuable." In these circumstances, your self-worth comes from the *outside*. And you are being controlled because whatever they think is "shameful" is directing your life instead of you acting from your *own* healthy conscience.

This outside shame or guilt may now even be in your head—you might have internalized it and even think it comes from you!

For example, if your parent or teacher was constantly putting you down, saying words or using body language indicating that you are not "adequate," this is a control mechanism. And you might have entered into a vicious circle trying to do things the "right way" in order to make *them* happy. This "making them happy" is, of course, impossible because they will always have new criticism for you!

This attempt by others to control you is a reflection of what is happening inside *them*. **It has nothing to do with you.** The reason they are critical usually comes from their own lack of self-acceptance, inner peace, and happiness. People who have inner peace and happiness do not criticize and attempt to control others. So, this really has nothing to do with YOU!

The next time someone acts like something you are doing is shameful or treats you as inadequate, ask yourself:

"Do *I* actually and truly and deeply feel that what I'm choosing, doing, or feeling is shameful or 'wrong'? Did this shame arise *from them*, or do I actually feel this action or choice is not aligned with my own deep self? Have I adopted someone else's standards?"

If someone has told you repeatedly that you are stupid or inferior, you might have started to believe this. Question these thoughts. Challenge them. They are not true, and they are not yours!

It's time to stop hiding or repressing real parts of yourself because *someone else* thinks what you are doing or feeling is shameful or wrong.

The very fact that you question all this will already loosen their grip on you, and you can begin your long road to rediscovering your true self and feeling "right" according to *you* and your true and perfect nature.

It's not easy to deal with shame. But there are things you can do that are helpful. For example, if you have been shamed a lot by a particular person, one way to confront this is to draw a picture of that person or even to just imagine them in front of you. Then you can engage in an imaginary role-play on your own or with a therapist.

As you look at the picture or visualize them in your mind, feel and express your anger at them for their unacceptable treatment. You can add body movements, yelling, drawing and shaking.

It is important to actually **feel the emotion in your body.** Do anything that feels natural to you to release this energy, so long as it is *without lashing out at them in person.*

And, of course, start to set boundaries and disallow any more shaming. Period.

There is a difference between someone telling you:

"When you don't shower, your body odor really bothers me," and,

"You are a disgusting person! Why can't you even take care of yourself?"

Can you *feel* the difference? One of these is simply a statement about the person's behavior and its impact on them, without a deep critical energy. The other attacks the other person, as if something is *wrong* with them on a deep level. It's an important distinction.

Any and all deep shaming of an individual is unacceptable. We don't need to learn to "tolerate this." We need to learn to express our boundaries and *not* tolerate it.

I don't feel we need to specify that we should not shame people for race, religion, gender, handicap, age, etc., **since all deep shaming of anyone is not okay.** So, no such list is needed.

I find that lists separate us into subcategories unnecessarily. These subcategories can be helpful to have support, encouragement, and to collaborate with others who have had similar experiences, due to their sexuality, gender, race or otherwise. But ultimately, people might start to identify *only* with the subcategory and forget that they belong to the bigger category of **human being.**

Being "Good Enough"

W HEN WE DON'T SEE OURSELVES as "good" or quite up to the standards of society or our parents, then we always need to fill in what we are "missing." We become needy, trying to feed off the outside world so they can affirm or reassure us that we are "okay."

We might buy fancy cars or clothes to try to feel better about ourselves or try to get a perfect house and a "respectable" job title. Maybe we live vicariously through our kids' achievements and try to always look a certain way for the world.

Well, what if you just felt good about your inner self... what would you STOP doing?

What if you already saw yourself as good? By just **BEING?** What if there's nothing wrong with you, nothing to improve, nothing to fix?

If you have formed a Courage Group, practice spending time together, sitting and doing nothing and giving each other permission to just **BE.**

As I mentioned earlier, I prefer the term "goodness" instead of "good enough." "Good enough" implies there's still a bad part of you, and you are settling for less. It's as if 80 percent of you is fine and 20 percent is bad, and that's "good enough," even if you are not 100 percent. I don't agree with this.

You are 100% goodness!

Your Inner Compass

You WERE BORN WITH A system—an inner compass—to guide you. This compass is comprised of your feelings, your gut, and your heart, and it tells you and *guides you* in what is true, what is good for you, and what isn't.

When you were young, did your parents (perhaps unintentionally) belittle, ignore, or invalidate your feelings? Were you put down, ignored, or invalidated if you cried? Were you shamed, guilted, threatened, or "trained" into displaying only certain feelings or behaviors?

Were you devalued and your worth not acknowledged? For example, were you only deemed to be "good" if you achieved high grades or excelled in sports? Were you too controlled? I am not talking about particular behaviors that might have been limited or restricted. I mean at a deeper level.

If so, then you might have **shut down or "deactivated" your inner compass** to survive. And now you constantly doubt yourself and only use your Calculator head.

In my view, this type of "parenting," which can pass from generation to generation, is not infused with unconditional love, trust, and acceptance. Rather, it reflects a *distrust* and *disrespect* of your inner being.

The Truth is painful. Feel it...

The beauty, however, is that **no one can actually remove, permanently disconnect, or disengage you from your inner system.** All that has happened is that you have pushed some things down or away...

Bring it all back up by starting to feel whatever comes up in you, and accepting and embracing **everything about you**.

Start to slowly trust your inner compass, even if no one ever has before.

Second-guessing

WHEN WE CONSTANTLY SECOND-GUESS OURSELVES, it's because we think there is a universal "right," "wrong," or "perfect" way of doing things. But this is not true; there is no single "right" path for all of us.

An urge to second-guess yourself might be a by-product of your upbringing. For example, did your parents doubt your decision-making abilities or put you down for "wrong" decisions as you were growing up? Did your childhood peers laugh at your activity choices? Is your spouse or boss always nitpicking at you or telling you that you can't do anything right?

Reminder: there is no universal right and wrong.

And no one has a crystal ball!

Slowly start to trust yourself and follow your joy. Follow what feels meaningful to you, no matter what others think.

As you begin to *trust yourself* and your decisions again, your inner tension will unravel.

Disappointing Others

"I'M SO DISAPPOINTED IN YOU..." Many of us have heard or seen this sentiment in the body language of others.

According to the *Oxford Dictionary,* disappointment is "the sadness or displeasure caused by the non-fulfillment of one's hopes or expectations." Well, if someone is disappointed in us, then we did not meet their expectations.

But what does that mean? What does it mean to have expectations? Why do others expect us to be a certain way? And why are we having such expectations of others?

If you are always afraid to disappoint others, then if someone makes even a tiny facial expression of disapproval in response to your behavior or choice, they end up immediately controlling you. If their body language or words are saying, "You are a disappointment," or they give you a cold look or raise an eyebrow, then you are immediately under their control. You are living in accordance with *their* expectations.

In fairness, can you also take a moment to see if you do this to others? Do you have firm expectations of others? Are you trying to control people?

Are you trying to control *life itself*?

Your Parenting

IT'S HARD TO REALIZE WHEN we are trying to control people or even life itself. We want things to happen our way right now. We want things *fixed* and we want it *right now.* This might also show itself in how we parent, constantly trying to "fix" our children and have rigid expectations of them.

It might be hard to admit that you could be acting like a dictator in your home. There is a good chance you are if your parents are or were. You might also be if you have not fully accepted yourself and your individuality. Dictatorships begin in the home and are expanded in the school system, in the government, and so on.

Are you trying to coerce your own children, if you have any, to be who you want them to be and to be a reflection *of you* to increase your own sense of self-worth or increase your own image in society? "If society decides that my son/daughter is awesome, then I must be awesome too!" Are you using your children to feel better about yourself?

I'm not talking about asking your kids to do chores. I'm not talking about encouraging them in school or to try different sports or art. I mean wanting them to **BE** a certain person, or you will not love them.

I am not trying to blame or criticize you. There are many understandable reasons why you might have fallen into this mode. I am just suggesting you inquire and reflect on whether this is *true* or not.

Are you constantly trying to "measure" or "fix" other people? How do you think it feels to have someone hovering over you all day to check and "adjust" you all day long?

Some of you might be objecting, saying it's all "for their own good" or even for their survival. Or you might object and insist that, even if you are pushing your kids to achieve goals you have set for them, or even if you expect them to be a certain way, you still love your children unconditionally.

Well, then, please consider how many conditions you are putting on this "love":

"I'll love you and *accept you more* if you become successful."

"I'll love you *more* if you take care of my needs."

"I'll love you *only if* you live your life a certain way."

I'm not saying you have to *agree* with all the choices or behaviors your children make. Your opinion might be different on many things... But when you have a difference in your opinion, **does your love remain steady in those moments?** While the two of you disagree about something? Even if you are in conflict? Do you still accept them in a deeper sense... or do you put them down and show that you are disappointed in them?

It's not about the specific action you take or the words you say. It's about *the feeling*.

It's about respect for their spirit, no matter where their path leads them and no matter how many "mistakes" you believe they are making at the moment.

Unconditional love means there are absolutely **NO conditions.** It means you love the person no matter what they say, do, or choose. It's really about the feeling you have inside you, and it can take many forms. It might even include refusing to see someone or setting boundaries while *still* loving them. What's important is that the action comes from a place of loving yourself and loving them, not from trying to control or punish them.

A friend of mine is absolutely full of love for her child who has fallen into using drugs, so she chose to set many boundaries, including temporarily putting her child out on the streets since he was not respecting her boundaries of certain behaviors in the home.

I do not doubt her level of love for herself or for the child. Both are clearly present, as far as I can sense.

Another friend does so much for her child, including buying many things, and is always "pleasing" them. It doesn't seem to me that this parent has unconditional love for the child. Perhaps they are guided by their own need to be liked and their own feelings of insecurity and unworthiness. In my opinion, it's not possible to love another fully while in that space. To truly love another, *a person must completely love themselves.*

And then there is the example of my son, who tutors and encourages and empowers so many children. He often starts his tutoring sessions by telling the children, "It's okay to fail," immediately relieving all their anxieties and giving them the acceptance that their parents often do not. He then uses many techniques to empower them. Of course, they end up building confidence and thriving in such an environment.

As a parent, I hope I have learned from my pain and my many mistakes. And I am still learning.

And I am currently encouraging my children to speak and follow their Truth.

"Your children are not your children. They are the sons and daughters of Life's longing for itself. They come through you but not from you, and though they are with you, yet they belong not to you. You may give them your love, but not your thoughts. For they have their own thoughts.

"You may house their bodies but not their souls, for their souls dwell in the house of tomorrow, which you cannot visit, not even in your dreams. You may strive to be like them but seek not to make them like you. For life goes not backward, nor tarries with yesterday." – Khalil Gibran

Giving and Getting
Unsolicited Advice

I AM SO "GUILTY" OF GIVING unsolicited advice. Even to this day, I still have to watch myself!

I used to think I was *helping* with my advice, but I've realized there can be a problem with the giving and getting of advice, especially if it's unsolicited.

Let me explain with an example of something I once heard someone do.

Let's say Person A is crying because they have lost a loved one, and Person B says, "You'll be fine. That person was old. It's part of life. You need to move on."

Well, as we already saw (I hope), **dismissing** the feelings and experience of Person A (which is what Person B has done) is disrespectful of the Truth of their being. So, ideally, the respectful and kind thing to do, in my opinion, is for Person B to **validate** Person A and give them space to cry and feel everything. This is a gift that respects the person and their humanity.

Now, once Person B has validated and given Person A space and support for them to process their feelings, should Person B now give them some advice?

It depends.

Most of the time, when the advice given is *unsolicited*, the impact on Person A can be the following:

- They may have *more* self-doubt; For example, maybe they felt they should take a month off work, and you tell them they *should not* do that. They now doubt their decision and decision-making ability—their inner compass.

- They may feel belittled, as if the advice-giver knows better than they do.
- The giving of advice may only serve the advice-giver (by encouraging their ego/superiority complex) rather than serving the receiver.

Overall, the message received might be the following:

"I don't think you know what you're doing. I don't trust your intuition."

The Truth is, Person B doesn't have enough information to give the unsolicited advice. They don't *know* the other person's whole life or everything they have gone through or what they feel. Only Person A does!

If you are interested to look at your advice-giving pattern, you may want to ask yourself these questions before giving any advice:

What is my honest intention when I am giving advice to someone else? Is it that I want to feel helpful, smart, and needed? To feel "valuable"? Or am I trying to solve other people's feelings quickly because I can't handle seeing someone feeling pain, or because of something else currently going on in my life? Or... am I truly trying to empower them?

It's best to generally only give advice when asked, expressly or implicitly, *and only if you really feel you understand their world and intend to empower them or give them a hand*. In other words, you are giving them advice not to "teach," or to solve something, but to support or inspire them to make their own moves. It is to encourage them to trust themselves, feel their emotions, be honest, and so forth.

And even after being asked for advice, you might start by asking them a lot of questions before dishing it out. For example:

Q. Why are you thinking of taking a month off work?
A. I'm feeling fed up.
Q. Oh really? In what way? What's going on?
A. My boss is really mean to me.
Q. That's rough. Do you want to share an example?
A. Yesterday, when I was late submitting a report he said, "You can't do anything right!"
Q. Gosh. You must have been hurt or mad when he said that.
A. Yes. I feel so depleted.
Q. Oh, I can imagine. What did you say afterwards?
A. Nothing.
Q. And how do you feel taking a month off will help you?
And so on.

Then perhaps you might realize they really have a good sense about what they need to do. Or, if you want to offer an opinion after the conversation, you can confirm by asking, "Do you want to hear my thoughts on this?"

Now, let's say the other person explicitly asked you for advice or agreed to receive it. Your advice would now be *solicited*. Let's also assume that you will not be giving the advice to feel better about yourself. Here are some things to think about:

Will you be hurt if they don't agree with your advice? Will the giving of the advice come back to being about *you* rather than about *them*? Can you handle it if they end up not taking your advice?

After all, they might not be ready for the action you are proposing or truth you are presenting.

Once you have clarified all this with yourself and are sure your intentions are clear, you can now follow your feeling and inner voice on what to say to a person at the moment they are seeking guidance.

And now, let's also take a moment to think about the reverse roles. How do *you* feel when someone keeps giving you advice all the time that you did *not* request? Can you set a loving boundary if it's not good for you or if you feel belittled, distrusted, or disempowered by this? My children have done this with me!

Mirrors Everywhere

WE CAN IMAGINE THE PEOPLE around us as mirrors. Those who can hold up a clear mirror simply reflect the Truth of who we are at that moment. This speaks to the importance of listening when someone else speaks instead of listening in order to reply. If we are *clear* mirrors, we are just listening and validating. This is the mirror of what is True.

But what if another person reflects something that's *untrue* due to their own confusion? Then we don't get an accurate reflection back of ourselves. So, we will need to be careful what we internalize when dealing with another human "mirror."

Let me give an example. If you are Person A and you say, "I'm afraid of lightning," **then this is the Truth.** After you express your Truth, several things can happen:

Option 1: Person B ignores, belittles, gaslights, or invalidates this Truth. The basic message they are sending to you is that your reality is wrong, shameful, not allowed, not right, not valuable, or not valid. They are unable or unwilling to hold up the mirror and reflect the Truth back to you. In other words, in their mind, your Truth does not *validly exist*. There is implicit shaming, intended or not.

Option 2: Person B immediately goes and "saves" Person A from the possibility of feeling uncomfortable or afraid by bringing them quickly indoors. To me, this is *not* helping. Person B has *some* clarity about the Truth (they see the others person's feelings), but they can't *handle* Person B's feelings. They can't handle and allow the Truth to be and are trying to fix and control and change the Truth.

So they can only hold up the mirror *for one split second*, then put it down quickly and try to fix and paint over the image, since they can't tolerate seeing the range of human emotions or Truth for a variety of reasons. This also gives the message to Person B that their feelings are not okay, that something is *wrong* with this picture.

This is not helpful to Person A, since Person B might be inadvertently giving Person A the message that there is something *wrong* with them, that they can't overcome or process this Truth and can't make decisions. Therefore, this "savior" Person B might actually be enabling, shaming, and *weakening* Person A in a way.

Person B does not see the *whole* Truth of Person B's experience and what is **possible** because they are still dealing with their own issues. Their behavior might even be helping them feel superior or boosting their own "self-esteem," or allowing them to avoid their own discomfort with emotions in general.

Option 3: Person B holds up the mirror and validates the True statement of Person A. They acknowledge and accept Person A's experience. They might nod with acceptance or can say something like the following to Person A: "You seem afraid. That must be hard for you. I understand completely because I'm also scared or used to be scared of ABC." They truly understand the other person's experience and allow them the time and space to process their feelings.

Person B can also give *solicited* advice or encouraging energy when needed. This acknowledges the Truth that Person A feels something, as well as the Truth that Person A can make choices, including asking for help. Person B might say, "What do you want to do? How can I support you? I used to take deep breaths and hum when I was scared of the dark. Would you like to try that?"

When others approach you with a personal topic, try to see which of these you typically fall into. Are you holding up a clear mirror for others?

If your son or daughter is sad or confused, does that help your image? Maybe not... so you might not accept this Truth and keep trying to "fix them" instead of allowing them their process.

Life is not a happiness competition. We must make room for all experiences, including sadness, anger, and grief.

Finally, take a moment to ask yourself if you are trying to control, manipulate, or influence others so you can see *yourself* in a certain way in *their* mirror. Do you want them to "like" you so you can look in their mirror, which will tell you, "You are a good and likable person." Trying to get others to "see" you how you want to be seen is actually manipulative and controlling, and will not serve you in the long run.

The same can be said If you try to *convince* another person to see and treat you a certain way because you are "worth it." Why do you need to convince them of this? So you can look at that mirror? It's not necessary: Just leave if they don't get it. Or do what you have to do. Just make your choices if the situation is not healthy for you.

You do not need to change anyone's mind or control their "mirror." Just look inside. Trust yourself.

And make your choices.

What's on the Inside
Is on the Outside

WHAT IS ON THE INSIDE will show itself on the outside and vice versa. So:

- If you are criticizing others, then you are likely criticizing yourself.
- If you are controlling others, then you are likely overly controlling yourself.
- If you are unkind to others, then you are likely unkind to yourself.

This also means that what others do to you or to others is often a reflection of what *they do to themselves.* (It doesn't mean we accept the behavior. It just means their behavior often has nothing to do with you. It's not personal.)

Given this Truth, beware of those that are sitting in shame—they will shame you because this is what they know and are dealing with. If they are critical of you, they are surely just as harsh on or unkind to themselves.

All this has nothing to do with you. Just focus on your own self-knowledge and Truth and on what *you* do and *why* you do it.

Knowing Yourself

IT SOUNDS ALMOST SILLY TO suggest you don't know yourself. Yet, this is exactly what I feel meditation is for and what so many philosophers have suggested we go about doing—getting to know ourselves deeply.

In my opinion, knowing oneself is personal work everyone needs to do if they are to form *healthy* relationships with others.

All relationships help us to learn about ourselves and to navigate our lives. But we can get stuck in unhealthy relationships if we keep denying or avoid dealing with an uncomfortable Truth, choosing to distract ourselves instead (with TV, alcohol, food, etc.).

My belief is that we are "growing" all the time. It is not true that we grow and become adults at eighteen, and that's it. Self-knowledge is a lifelong process of experiencing, expanding, learning about, and understanding ourselves.

And this growing is actually literal if you start to feel your energy. You actually "expand" beyond your height and width, in terms of energy, just like a candle exists and illuminates beyond its flame.

Control and Beliefs

WHY DO OUR RELIGION, FAMILY and society try to exert so much control through their rules, often accompanying the breaking of the rules with shaming? This puts people down and keeps them easily manipulatable.

What would happen if religion or rules were not around to control us? Many of us have been taught that if there were no rules, then we would be "evil" or "sinners," so we actually think *we need* the control or else we will be dangerous or evil!

I certainly don't believe that! We don't need to be afraid of ourselves! When we are free, have processed our pain and healed, we are good and loving as free souls and human beings.

All this time, we have been living under the impression that to be "accepted" we have to make our decisions based on *outside* rules, controls, religion, and peer pressure.

But what if you start to be guided by the inside? From your inner knowing and compass? At times, doing this might not be easy, and there can be "repercussions." There will be many that do not agree with you and your choices.

Knowing this, which one will you choose? It's a choice between being truly alive versus *not* being truly alive. Choosing the life of the *fake you* is the death of the *true you* (and vice versa).

It's time to resuscitate the real you!

You may encounter some rocky roads, but choosing the *true you* with its rocky roads can still be the right path for you! Have faith that, no matter what happens in your life, you can always make some kind of choice.

I believe in Y♥U.
Keep opening up!

Starting To Feel Alive

Feeling Everything

IF YOU ARE READY TO feel fully alive, then naturally, you need to start to feel life and **be in it and not somewhere else!** This means:

- Starting to feel and allow all your emotions to be felt, since they are here.
- Learning to feel everything around you since it is here.
- Expressing yourself from the heart, not the head.
- Understanding and feeling your power of choice instead of trying to control others.
- Slowly learning to move with, not against, life. Moving with life means not always living in anticipation. (If you are always thinking and worrying about the future, then you are in the Calculator head instead of being here in reality.)

This way of living allows your inner creativity and essence to slowly start expressing itself *in whatever way it will*. Just follow your nature and your essence will flow.

But don't assume this flow is necessarily fun or painless. It could be messy and difficult and may still be **your right path!**

We are on a journey of finding ourselves, of listening to our "soul" or essence. Each person needs to find their own "mission" or way of living. And it's not really one mission. *It is a constant way*—a way of being and doing—*from the source of you.*

For example, most of this book is writing itself. I don't have to overthink what it's going to be! Over time, the contents of this book are simply *flowing* from my pain, from my heart, and my inner knowing onto the paper. Liquid flowing and spilling out. I guess that is why they call it "flow," because there is no hesitation, no doubts, no insecurity. **Just simple Truth from the soul, as it shows itself.**

What is *your* soul crying out to do? Where do you feel a moment of flow and no overthinking? Find it, don't judge it, and follow it.

Follow your *true you* every moment of the day.

Why Predict the Outcome Before You Act?

LET'S SAY YOU HAVE A strong pull, gut feeling, or drive from deep inside to do something—call one of your teachers, go to a workshop, visit a specific country or person. You don't know exactly why or exactly what will happen. So you hesitate.

Why do you always need to know exactly why or what the result will be? Are you trying to see if it makes sense? To see if it feeds the ego or other people's expectations? Are you trying to predict everything based on your past experience? Your past experience is very limited!

What if you simply *follow* this intuition, this gut feeling, this "deeper you," without knowing the exact end result or the outcome?

What if you just trust?

If you only do things for the **anticipated result,** then you are deeply limiting your existence, since we cannot know the result of what we do. We cannot predict the exact impact or outcome!

For example, let's say you have a curiosity and desire to call a teacher you feel some connection with to ask for career advice.

Your Calculator head might say, "Well, what will happen? What's the point? What if they think I'm weird if I call? Maybe it's inappropriate for me to call."

Then your Calculator might name five possible outcomes based on past experiences and you might decide what to do only based on those five experiences, even though your prediction is so limited by your past!

Your heart/gut/soul, if you listen, might say, "I really feel curious to do this, and so I will. Who knows what is going to happen when I do... and it doesn't matter! I'm doing it anyway because I have a gut feeling to do it. Let's see what happens."

Who knows if a sentence the teacher will say will remind us of some past painful experience which encourages us to deal with it? Who knows if they will say something to inspire us to another path? Who knows! **The mere fact of this openness allows many more possibilities to occur** since we are not looking for specific outcomes only. The fact of being open actually changes the experiences that are possible!

So stop overanalysing and overthinking everything and limiting your life. If you are following a dance partner in salsa or tango, do you always think and anticipate the next move? Do you refuse to make a move until you know the next 30 steps coming? No, you don't. So now, just imagine your intuition/universe/life is your dance partner. Life is dancing with you and guiding you. You are dancing with the universe! That's your partner! **Follow that part of you.**

The way we are all connected is by all having the same "partner" to dance with! It's almost like we have a higher voice that interacts with our unique voice... it's magic!

When you sit quietly in meditation and keep asking yourself a question, the answer *does* come. It is quiet, and it is clear. Listen to it. The answer might be out of your comfort zone, but it *is* in your "truth zone."

There is a real inner calm that comes from listening to what feels clear inside and doing it **without knowing the exact why or outcome**.

This listening to self can be a long feeling that stays—for example, constantly gravitating towards art or dance. Or it can be on the spot—a feeling of wanting to explore or learn about a subject.

When was the last time you just **listened to yourself** and followed your inner voice without knowing the exact result?

Maybe try to take a walk without knowing the end result and just turn left and right as you feel like it, following "whatever"—a beautiful road; a bird. Follow your curiosity. Follow what feels next on this path. Can you feel the freedom and joy of this listening?

Soon, listening within will become normal, and your soul will be free to live.

Follow you. And only you.

You are fed by a magnificent
energy from beyond!

The End of Striving

CAN YOU PUT ASIDE YOUR effort to be someone you're not for a moment, and instead, look for what feels easy and natural to you?

If your true self loves to listen to music alone, so be it.
If you are drawn to try graffiti art, so be it.
If you love to bake, so be it.
If you are called to read, so be it.
If you feel like being an activist, so be it.
If you are called to learn a new language or subject for no "practical" reason, so be it.
If you feel like trying mountain climbing, so be it.

None of these actions are better than the other. In every moment, we exist and can follow whatever feels right.

You already know your nature. It may be covered up a bit (or perhaps you have set it aside), but it's *not gone*. Remove the resistance and the striving, and you will see what is "easy" and natural. "Easy" doesn't mean you won't struggle or work your butt off for months or experience pain... but it might, for example, be easier for you to speak up and face a difficult situation than to remain silent.

And if your personal relationships are not compatible with what you feel and need to do? Then you might need to rethink those relationships.

Trusting Life

LET'S ASSUME THERE IS A *flow of life*, like a positive wind force or current encouraging all things in the right direction... this "wind" is trying to move you in a certain direction using your feelings and intuition. If you **resist** by ignoring your senses, feelings, and intuition, you might develop anxiety because all this resistance is moving you **in the wrong direction for you**.

Or it leaves you just feeling stuck.

So why are you resisting? Because it's scary, because it's an unknown direction? Because it's painful? Because you do not trust yourself or life? Because those around you did not trust you?

You have a **choice**.

Trust the flow of life. The wind beneath your wings, in your sails... and your inner compass. It might be painful, unknown, or scary, but it might still be the "right" way for your life. Go there, and see what happens.

> "You're a leaf scattered by an invisible wind.
> Don't you know something is moving you?"
> – Rumi

Listening to Your Inner Compass

BEFORE I BECAME GOOD AT listening to myself, I was not sure what this meant. I was listening to a talk about "listening within," and so I decided to sit and try to figure out what this meant.

I sat alone often, in meditation, one might call it, but I still felt completely lost and desperate for a variety of reasons. Nothing felt okay in my life or in my relationships. I was in so much distress and, in this desperation, I decided I'd try to ask the universe, life, or my intuition (anything or anyone!) the following questions:

"What should I do?"
"What should I be?"

I sat and listened, and my "intuition" answered me. This quiet and clear inner voice said:

"Be quiet."

At first, I laughed. The "universe" wants me to shut up!

But then I decided to actually listen to this advice! So I sat with myself a lot after that. In pain, in confusion, in anything and everything.

Meditation connects us with the deeper us, behind our thoughts. It can help us get in tune with **the body, soul, and life energy.** From there, we can begin to be sincere with ourselves.

And, in that silence, I eventually made a choice. My choice was to start to **speak my Truth.**

And that's what I have been doing ever since.

This choice has caused so much turmoil, hurricanes, disruptions, stress, and relationship transformations... but also a lot of peace in my inner world. Because doing so feels **right to me.** And I now feel I am more aligned with the path I should be on. Who said getting back on the right track would be painless?

What does it mean to live and speak your Truth? It means you are attuned to your heart and trusting the voice within as your compass.

The fact you're very unhappy in something (job, relationship, living situation) doesn't mean something is wrong *with you.* It might mean it's wrong *for you.*

Start listening to yourself at a deeper level and nourish this inner freedom. We can't just listen to the outside world and other people's preferences, priorities, and expectations that make us go against what **we know is best for us**! We need to listen to ourselves; we need to listen to our souls. The answer is to trust that which is within you.

> Stop fighting yourself—that's the
> opposite of inner peace.

Listen deeply, and you will know what to do. You may not always *like* what this inner voice tells you... but if it keeps saying the same thing and if it is clear, quiet, and resolved, it's likely your Truth.

There is a saying, "Emotions are all divine." That's because they come from the heart. So start by listening to all of them. They are part of the essence of being human, and are intertwined with the Truth of Life. And from this place of Truth can come clarity and resolve. From there can come *an action that is right for you.*

It might take a leap of faith, and that's why we need Courage and Trust at that very instant. But things will come together.

> "You can solve any problem by just sitting down on the floor." – My daughter, at age twelve

Curiosity

CURIOSITY DOESN'T WANT ANYTHING AND is a great challenger to our Calculator head, the "thief" that robs us of living.

Curious thoughts (as opposed to critical/Calculator thoughts) are the opposite of fear and require no energy. And, they lead us to Truth.

When you are curious, you are naturally driven without criticism. You are looking for Truth vs. untruth instead of what's "good or bad." You are not judging. You are open to seeing the Truth and not blocked by what you *want* to see.

So, if you keep your mind in a curious disposition and *aim to see the Truth,* even if it's painful, you'll be in a very open state!

Use curiosity to inquire about your feelings. Let's say you feel sad. You can be curious and find out *why.* But be careful, there are two different types of "why," even with the same question, and we want to steer away from the **Critical Why** and go towards the **Curious Why.**

Critical Why: "Why am I feeling sad? I *shouldn't* be upset since it's not a big deal." This has a critical tone. It sucks your energy and doesn't help you understand yourself or the Truth or what you need. And by speaking to yourself this way, you avoid feeling the sadness, and it's still there. You are stuck.

Curious Why: "Why am I feeling sad? I wonder why I'm feeling this way. Am I lonely? Do I need to try to make new friends? Do I need time to process sadness or grief?" Curiosity with a self-compassionate tone is effortless and moves you in the right direction towards self-understanding and self-knowing and perhaps getting help or other needs met.

Notice all of your "whys." If they are **Critical Whys,** then they do not help you.

Can you be curious instead and be willing to see the Truth, no matter what? Only when we accept the Truth can we move forward from a place of reality. And we are not living in reality when we live **in denial.**

Again, this can stem from having grown up in a dysfunctional family. A dysfunctional family is one that **denies painful feelings,** and it disorients everyone involved. Sweeping things under the rug or pretending issues don't exist, like addiction or violence in the home, are a recipe for insecurity, uncertainty, and self-distrust, because the perceptions don't match what others are acting like in the house.

So, stop pretending everything is normal when it's not. It causes self-doubt, pain, and anxiety.

Let's face and live in reality, whatever it is, as much as possible. **Only from reality can you make choices from a place of Truth.**

What Are You "Addicted" To?

WHAT IS GIVING YOU TEMPORARY relief from the stress or pain you feel? Or serving as a temporary escape? For example:

- Drinking alcohol
- Binge-watching TV
- Over-exercising
- Overeating
- Putting too many hours into work
- Cleaning endlessly.

Addiction is often a mechanism we use to deal with trauma or to help escape feelings and pain. And it is understandable, as it serves a protective purpose for overwhelming times. But it only provides temporary relief and does not address the real issue. To heal, we will need to see and face the wounds within.

Are you avoiding looking at past pain, hurt, or fears of rejection? You might, for example, be doing a million different things just to get a "hit" of approval or positive reinforcement.

This might be hard to see! After performing an action, you might just think, "Oh, I did something nice for someone, and so I feel good about myself for a moment!" But it's only for a moment because deeply, you do not truly feel good inside... and you will find yourself needing to get another "hit" as soon as the short-lived feeling of relief passes.

Instead of continuing this pattern, you can choose to sit and allow your feelings so that you are able to heal your wounds and pain. Start by asking yourself, **"Why do I have pain?"** And get support if you need help to deal with your pain.

You have taken the first step and are on your way!

Anger

FEELING ANGER CAN SOMETIMES BE healthy to get us out of fear, apathy, grief, shame, and unhealthy relationships or situations. It gives us the **ENERGY** to set a boundary and take care of ourselves.

Anger is a natural and healthy emotion.

For centuries, women, in particular, have been taught not to get angry. Men have been brutalized and told not to allow or express their feelings, including anger, in a healthy manner.

It is healthy to look inside when we become angry so we can know what choices to make and what boundaries we need to set or actions we need to take.

For example, maybe you get angry when someone yells at you, and so, if you realize and understand this, you can express your boundary and ask them to stop communicating in this way to you. Or maybe you take some other boundary-related action. Or maybe you are angry about your situation and simply realize, "Hey, I matter!"

Your healthy anger is *telling you* that something is not okay.

If you find yourself feeling angry, take some time alone and listen to it clearly. Then decide what you need to do for yourself. This is how anger, self-love, and Courage can sometimes intertwine!

But what happens if you feel guilt and shame around your emotion of anger? What if you always say, "I *shouldn't feel* upset." "I *shouldn't feel* mad at my teacher; she's just trying to help." "I *shouldn't feel* mad about what my friend said. All teenagers talk like that, and she helps me often." "I *shouldn't feel* mad at a parent; they supported me." If you dismiss your emotions, you are not only controlled by the outside but by the inside as well.

You are allowed to feel angry about whatever you feel angry about!

You are allowed to feel angry even at your parents—even if they "did their best."

It's all allowed.

I'm not talking about actions such as lashing out, being aggressive or violent. I'm just discussing the importance of allowing the *feeling* of anger. Anger and aggression are not the same and have been incorrectly equated. Anger is a feeling, and aggression is an action. Between the feeling and the action, there is **choice**. I am certainly a proponent of taking space and knowing how to calm ourselves down in these situations to see why we are upset and to **choose** what we would like to do.

Sometimes, however, when our anger makes no sense to us, we might need to look deeper and will often find hurt underneath the anger. So, anger can actually have a vulnerable element to it that we may need to understand in ourselves better.

We might also find other Truths when noticing our anger. Perhaps we come to recognize we are critical and nitpicking at others (and therefore at ourselves). Or perhaps we might come to realize we are angry at the wrong person because we were not allowed, or it wasn't safe to feel anger at the correct person who actually hurt us.

Be open to seeing all Truths!

All feelings are positive because they are True and part of a person's inner compass.

There are no negative emotions.

So, you are allowed to feel mad, you are allowed to feel hurt, you are allowed to feel upset. Once you allow for the feeling, then figure out *why* you are feeling this way and perhaps find a healthy way to process or express it.

We are practising **feeling** and expressing, but, again, this is not the same as **lashing out at someone.**

If you constantly get mad because you don't get what you want or you want people to do what you want, and lash out when they don't, your emotion might just be an issue of control or perfectionism—wanting and expecting everything to go your way, which is something you might need to work through, rather than about setting healthy boundaries.

Feeling our anger is not about hurting others, controlling others, or lashing out. The intention matters!

Feeling angry and deciding to express and hold a boundary for the right reasons is a powerful move towards your natural path.

People Who Challenge Your Reality

THIS "LIVING IN REALITY" OR Truth that I have been trying to describe in this book is particularly difficult to do if we are in a relationship with someone who is controlling, manipulative, or denying our reality. It can lead to us being in judgment of ourselves, overthinking, and simply having difficulty being in reality. We can have a hard time feeling our own essence.

For example, if every time you have a feeling and share it with your partner or parent, they deny, dismiss, or gaslight this reality, your mind may begin to question if it is okay for you to have these thoughts or feelings in the first place. And so you try to deny or suppress the thoughts and feelings more yourself, which creates further self-doubt—which keeps you hidden, small, and insecure. It can lead to all kinds of mental health issues.

Identify those around you who are constantly denying the feelings and reality of others, overtly or subtly. You might need to learn to assert yourself and maybe even remove yourself temporarily or permanently from the situation or relationship.

It might be time for you to set a boundary. This is what your anger and inner compass are for. For you.

There is huge power in saying NO. It means...

I exist. I matter.

Your Boundaries Are You!

BOUNDARIES ARE NOT JUST RULES you put on others. This is a big misunderstanding of the word. Boundaries are essentially about *being you*. Their purpose is actually to define you as a separate person from others. In other words, it's where you stop and others start, like a fence that separates different gardens. Boundaries lead to authenticity and individuality.

It's very difficult to figure out who you are if there are no boundaries in your home. Without boundaries, people get merged, enmeshed, and are unable to live as individuals. You don't know what's *your* feeling vs. what's *their* feeling. You operate as a pair or group, and it's unhealthy! Even a simple idea like, "We all love skiing," or "We are a loud family" gives me signals that each person has not learned what they *personally* feel. Perhaps they have adopted a group mentality due to pressures to do so or habits formed generations ago.

> Healthy relationships include respect
> for each person's boundaries.

Start by asking what **feels okay to you**. It's not too late to start. You know your boundaries. For example, you might want to say, "It's not okay with me if you yell," or "I'm too tired to speak today," and so on. Boundaries are an expression of your "okay."

They can be temporary and change with time, depending on what you are currently experiencing or are able to handle.

A healthy boundary is just an expression of, "what is okay with me and what is not okay." Their main purpose is *to allow you to define yourself*—so you become and act like YOU and not as others think or want you to be. Your intention should not be to control the other person. It should be to **respect your inner self**.

Identifying and naming that something happened that was not okay for you is not blaming. Nor is it being a victim. It is an **act of self-love.** When you act from a place of honoring and listening to yourself and with self-love, you become one with the flow of life. **Your body will "speak" and be in "dis-ease" if you do not listen.**

Do not be afraid that if you set a boundary, this means you do not love the other person. This is not true.

Love isn't taking abuse. Self-love and even loving others means setting boundaries on toxic behaviors. One day, you might decide to forgive and understand, and maybe the person might even help themselves by having seen your mirror and feedback. But first, set the boundary, **because you love and care about yourself**.

Having healthy boundaries from a place of self-love does not only help you; it also helps the world! For example, if you don't allow someone to put you down, it means **you matter.** This is something that is not only good for you but also good for the world! If you live in a healthy way, you are becoming a positive player in the world in myriad ways, which will manifest over time.

Setting this healthy boundary can also impact the person who put you down and, by extension, their family. Perhaps they might think twice about this behavior and not do it in the future (so their family will no longer be exposed to it).

Or, for example, if you don't allow a codependent individual to enact their behaviors with you, you might be taking them one step closer to getting help. This is not in your control, of course, but it might end up a natural consequence of you expressing your boundaries.

Boundaries and Control

WHEN YOU SET A BOUNDARY, the intention matters! You are not putting rules into effect for the sake of controlling people, situations, or behavior. You are not trying to say, "My rules are better than yours," or "You have to do something." That's not what boundaries are about.

If someone yells and you set a boundary of not yelling at you, you are basically saying, "This is not okay with me given where I am at, at this moment."

You do so from a place of *self-love* and *self-knowing*. It's not so you can *control* the other person. If you have very sensitive ears, you might even say, "I can't speak for more than five minutes if it's louder than a whisper." There is no wrong or right boundary. It's really what feels okay to you, so you take care of yourself and live true to you! It has nothing to do with the other person.

Therefore, you are not against the person; you are *for you*. This is a very important difference!

If you tell someone that yelling is not okay, and they keep doing it, and if you now expect the person to "comply" with your rules, well, that's controlling.

So, instead, if they don't respect your boundary—for example, they keep insulting or yelling and plowing through the boundaries you've set—you will need to make more choices. Choose to leave the room and explain this again another time. You can choose to get help for the relationship with a therapist, you can choose to leave the relationship, or you can choose another route that feels appropriate to you.

I'm not saying the choices here are easy. I'm saying **you can make choices**. And that you are responsible for your own life. You cannot force anyone to change or see their behavior differently. Do not spend years and years trying to convince them.

You are not "right," and they are not "bad." You are just clear about what you feel is right for you right now, given your inner compass.

Make your choices for you, and let things play out as they play out.

True boundaries are hard to set and express, and major Courage is often necessary, especially if you have never set boundaries with anyone.

You will need to HOLD YOUR GROUND—literally.

Being Grounded

FEELING ALL OF OUR EMOTIONS, having the Courage to set boundaries, and looking for our inner intuition—this is not easy stuff! What does the earth, *the ground,* have to do with it? Well...

Do you believe in gravity?

Seems like a crazy question. But did you ever actually take a moment to not only feel gravity but *to trust* gravity? To experience that the earth is actually *holding* you?

Why does this matter? Because if you feel unstable physically, if you are all in your head and can't feel your body, and especially your feet and the ground, then imagine how this affects you. Compare this to a person who **feels the ground**!

The more you get in touch with the earth with different meditations, grounding, barefoot walking, and other similar practices, the more stable you will feel.

Here's a meditation you can use so you can get more in touch with the earth. Practice standing with your eyes closed and imagine your feet are like magnets. Sway to feel the magnetic field connecting your center with the earth.

Do not read this and try to just absorb this intellectually; that's useless. **Everything needs to be felt in the body.** Thinking or intellectualizing about it isn't enough; this needs direct somatic experience (feeling it). That's what matters.

With regular practice, we start to feel "held" and less unbalanced, and therefore don't need to hold on to everything else so tightly.

All meditations and practices where you feel the body and the ground will help ground you. This is no small thing when it comes to making us feel better. It's so as not to feel like we are floating in the air, unstable, about to fall, unsafe. So we can literally feel on the ground!

Each person needs to find their own practice that helps them reconnect with the earth.

This practice also helps us release our thoughts and "ground us," just like electricians do with electrical systems. We can ground ourselves when our head is overheated and overthinking. I am not using this as an analogy but *literally* as a matter of physics and electromagnetism—just as we ground electricity in our homes.

Practice the earthing meditation mentioned above as often as you can, especially when you feel fine or just a slight disturbance, so you can experience its power and learn to feel yourself deeply. Of course, it's also very useful if you are feeling overwhelmed.

Inhale: Focus on energy from the earth rising inside you; open your heart.

Exhale: Allow the energy to descend (surrender to the earth) to create grounding.

> *"There are a thousand ways to kneel and kiss the ground; there are a thousand ways to go home again." – Rumi*

Resentment

Boundaries can be helpful and necessary to define and protect us, but they do not remove the pain if you perceive you have not been treated well. You might be angry and hurt, and of course, this is allowed, since all feelings are allowed.

But if you keep holding on to this past hurt and not letting it go, then you might find yourself sitting in resentment, which will hold you back from living.

So, what can you do?

Try to see how you contributed to this "wrong," even if your contribution amounts to only *one* percent! For example, you might come to acknowledge that you didn't set boundaries, thus inadvertently giving a sort of "permission" to be disrespected by the other person. Your one-percent acknowledgment here can help loosen the grip resentment has on you!

You can also try to share your pain with the person and perhaps they can acknowledge and apologize. But sometimes the other person is not able or ready to do so. I understand that sometimes we want the other person to see our pain and to be accountable; in other words, we want some justice. But then ask yourself, "Is this even *possible*, especially if they do not see their own pain?"

If they can't understand and validate your hurt, then it might help to role-play or to write letters to the person without ever sending them. Some call these "burn letters," and they can help release old pain and heal old wounds.

You can also use *compassion* to help you get past this. If you can see that they are suffering, then maybe you can also see that what they did wasn't personal. It wasn't really about *you*. Perhaps they were going through something and were not consciously trying to hurt you.

And, of course, you can always seek help. Perhaps read and engage in trauma work, where you physically re-enact events in life in your imagination and in your body in order to resolve them.

Follow what works for you and as usual, **listen to your body, which is your guide.**

What matters most is to realize that you are sitting in resentment. Then, instead of ruminating on what they've done, give some attention to what you can do NOW to take care of yourself and stop suffering!

Haven't you suffered enough?

Blame and Punishment

WHEN WE RESORT TO BLAME, control, and punishment, this leads us to think that the other person is "bad." We think we cannot be happy until they get what they deserve. They hurt us and therefore, *deserve* to be hurt.

This is false.

They do NOT deserve hurt. They deserve good things, love, and understanding.

In my view, if we adopt a "they are bad" concept, this also means that *we* still feel powerless and that *we* have not come to see our own self-worth.

Deep blaming or punishment of another fails to respect their humanity and their goodness, *and thus yours.* They go hand in hand.

Our POWER lies in loving ourselves and showing love to others by empathizing and NOT punishing. Rather, we can set loving boundaries. There is a *big* difference.

Setting loving boundaries has an intention that is *not about punishing or controlling.* When we love ourselves, we don't need to control others to feel powerful or to feed our sense of ego. We already feel our inner power and feel comfortable in our own skin.

Be aware of the energy in yourself and in others: Do you blame, control, or punish others, or just set boundaries? **Look at the intent behind the action.** For example, if you are mad during a conversation and tell someone, "I can't talk to you right now," are you giving someone the "silent treatment" (which is passive-aggressive and used as an attempt to control or punish), or are you just protecting your integrity and need of space (which is self-love and power without being *against* the other person or trying to hurt or control them).

A tendency to blame and punish others is a reflection of *what you do to yourself*. In other words, you are likely also blaming yourself deeply.

So, before you work on not blaming or punishing others, **start with yourself!**

In this book, I often speak about needing to feel your pain from an event. But this is not the same as **causing your own punishment, suffering, or self-sabotage!** Are you choosing to stay in a situation that causes you pain, or failing to do something else because you don't feel deserving of love, happiness, or freedom from suffering?

And if someone else is blaming you or punishing you, do you accept this? Do you feel you *deserve it,* or do you set a boundary?

Having healthy boundaries and not **accepting or inflicting** blame and punishment drives the world to a better place where people are innately valued.

It starts with you.

Compassion

COMPASSION MEANS UNDERSTANDING AND KINDNESS—SIMPLY understanding why a person feels what they feel or did what they did. It can be as simple as understanding why we are sad, or someone else is. Or it can be understanding the suffering that led someone to commit a crime.

Understanding someone or their "bad" behavior or action should not be confused with *excusing* or *allowing* that behavior. For example, I might understand why someone is yelling. They are mad, frustrated, hurt, or feeling alone, and I feel for them. And they are *allowed* to be mad and to feel, period.

But while I can understand their frustration, it doesn't mean I would sit there and allow them to yell at me or continue to be around them. I would express my boundary and make choices, but it is not *against them* because I understand them. It is about their **behavior.**

So, I am not *against* their person, their essence, their being. I'm just against *the choice* they made at this moment—how they acted out. And I am also *for* me since I feel for myself.

Doing this is very powerful. There is **no need for bad spirit in play** because someone has behaved in an unacceptable way. I understand that something has led to this, and I know that if I had many years to sit with them and understand their whole life, I could "get" why they are behaving this way.

So I refuse to be hard on them. Because doing so implies that I am hard on myself, which I also refuse to do.

This is because I understand myself.

Accountability

LEARNING TO BE MORE SELF-COMPASSIONATE and less harsh or critical doesn't mean living in denial, making excuses, or avoiding our own responsibility. Quite the opposite, actually!

In my experience, people often avoid accountability for their actions. They think accountability means "faultiness," "failing," or "being defective," and thus avoid having to *go there*.

And so their automatic reaction is to blame someone else, point the finger, or make some excuse, no matter what happens!

Anything other than taking responsibility.

This is understandable, given that we are raised in societies where people get *punished* or are *devalued* as soon as they take responsibility (whether we look at our criminal justice system or the workplace). But, as we already saw, exerting punishment or being harsh on a person, which is not the same as holding them accountable, doesn't respect the person who caused the harm and their basic dignity.

It is also very hard for a person to take responsibility for their actions and mistakes if their ego, perfectionism, or other fears do not allow it, because it will reduce the "score" they keep track of in order to have evidence of how "good" they are. They cannot be accountable if doing so causes them to feel deep shame. All societal punishing, shaming, and guilting attitudes perpetuate this view of accountability as being shameful or "losing a point" on the value scale.

Instead of all this harshness, we can all choose to be kind to ourselves.

When you start to really and truly understand yourself, there is no way to be hard on yourself because you understand and *feel for yourself*. This understanding makes you kind toward yourself and eventually makes you naturally kind towards others. That's why, as I know I've mentioned so many times, **it all starts with self.**

So, whether there is a small misstep, a tiny mistake, or a bigger one, we start by *separating the behavior from the person*. This is imperative and will help to remove all the perfectionist and ego issues and allow accountability to occur.

The inner voice says, "I made a mistake," vs. "I am a horrible, stupid, useless human being."

When someone else has acted in a way that has caused you pain, you can also "hold them accountable" without blaming, attacking, or punishing them.

Simply speak your Truth and act according to it without attacking.

Nothing else is needed. Your Truth is in the world, and things will adjust themselves.

For example: Let's say I'm mad because Person A did something which I felt was hurtful. I can choose to express myself to them and let it be known that I am upset over their behavior.

From here on, I'll take responsibility for my life and not try to control them.

My intention is not to attack the other person deeply for their action or behavior. I am hurt and simply do not accept their *behavior*—this has nothing to do with their inner person. I still believe in that person and their humanity. Maybe they have been abused. Who knows what they've gone through? I'm not concerned with that right now. I'm just acting from a place of my own self-love.

Holding someone accountable is never punishing or *deep*. Punishment implies *they* are bad. It is really not the same as, "You did a behavior or made a mistake that I find unacceptable for me." There is a BIG difference.

Once you feel this difference, you develop compassion, first for yourself and then for others.

You learn to allow yourself mistakes, to see your mistakes, and to take responsibility for them without attacking yourself on a deep human level. You become accountable to yourself!

But the more ego and self-worth issues you have, the more likely you will punish yourself and others instead of simply being accountable, setting your loving boundaries, taking responsibility for your own choices, and holding others accountable with empathy.

Now, some of you might think this accountability thing is about being compassionate and kind, but actually, it's also about POWER.

Accountability is a powerful move, not a weak one.

If someone cannot take responsibility for their behavior and life, this leads to an inability to see **their power of choosing altogether!** They think life always "happens to them." They will always look for someone to blame or to take responsibility for a mistake, so they remain **powerless in all aspects of their life.**

If you choose accountability no matter what happens, then you are actually *looking* for how *you* participated (not blaming yourself) in the event in some way, or what *you* can do or what *you* can learn. Instead of "this happened to me," you are able to see how you "chose" or participated in this in some way, or what you can choose now or what can learn from this now.

And with these "accountability glasses" on at all times, we start to see how much we are **actually choosing all the time!**

Accountability is a powerful move because it means you are an actor in the world and in your life and can have an impact. You make things happen.

It doesn't matter if you made a "mistake." The point is that you realize you have **the power of choice**. That's why accountability is always a power move.

This is the way to live in your power and encourage others to do the same instead of feeling like a victim of life.

Now please... if you actually get this point or agree... there is no need to go around getting angry at, controlling, or demeaning someone you perceive as "being a victim." This kind of anger is controlling behavior. Everything and everyone has its time, and it took you time to get to this moment.

So, if you want to be a gentle and compassionate guide, that's great. But I doubt that person needs more criticism. That will not help them see anything!

Learning From Your Teachers

THE WORD "TEACHER" IS OFTEN equated with a person standing in front of a class of students. How far that is from the Truth!

Everyone and everything is a teacher. Every relationship is a teacher, every tear from your eyes is a teacher, and every movement of a branch in the wind is a teacher.

No matter what happens, we can always ask the question:

"What am I to learn from this?"

We are not diving into guilt or beating ourselves up for being in a bad situation, and I am certainly not encouraging thoughts like, "What did I do to deserve this?" What I'm talking about is Truth-based, *curious* type of questions you can ask yourself, such as:

"What am I to learn from this? To take care of myself? That I matter? That I am people-pleasing too much?"

Try to see *your part* in every situation. This is not self-blame but accountability. You might try to understand, for example, how you might be feeding a problem with the choices you make, then realize you can make different choices! That's your power!

"Do *I* need to learn to set boundaries, and is this person or situation *I'm* upset with serving my purpose and Truth? Or... do *I* need to learn not to see everything as personal? Do *I* need to learn not to keep on making everything about me? Do *I* need to learn to speak up for other people who live this situation?"

For each and every frustration, ask, "What am *I* supposed to learn from this? What am I **meant to do** in this situation?"

Notice that every question that's just been posed uses an "I," so the answer and responsibility is **internal**.

It's hard to see every moment and every pain as a lesson... but that's often what they are. And they are there to redirect you to your better path.

Remember, no matter where you are or what you're doing, you have the internal compass to guide you on which way to go. The more you listen to your compass, the clearer things become, and the more you will be on your way to your true, peaceful life.

There are no predetermined paths, but if you listen to your deepest self, all paths will lead to the same place of sitting in Truth.

Embrace everything and everyone as a teacher. But beware of *following* teachers or gurus! Although we can learn from everyone, ultimately, the compass you need to follow...

is your own.

Forgiveness Starts with You

FORGIVING OTHERS BEGINS WITH UNDERSTANDING and forgiving yourself for everything.

Everything.

For it is only when you see your own mistakes, understand and love yourself fully regardless, and are no longer hard on yourself that you can forgive another person.

As we saw, if you are still stuck in perfectionism, you might have a difficult time with this process.

Are you ready to accept your mistakes and your humanity? Can you apologize to the other party and forgive yourself? Can you have compassion for yourself, knowing that it probably happened because you were overwhelmed or dealing with other hardships? Are you truly being accountable for your actions? Does this misstep or behavior make your *essence* imperfect or make you a "bad person"?

Perfectionism—striving for life and all of your behavior to be perfect—versus *being goodness* inside will affect your ability to forgive.

If you see yourself as perfectly fine inside *but human in terms of behavior and learning,* then you understand that we are all perfect in our essence and are just living out life's experiences and trying to navigate it!

However, if you criticize yourself, then **you still do not understand your whole history that led to this moment.** If you stay in this perfectionist mode, you might be critical of yourself, want life and your behavior to be perfect, and be unable to move out of the fear of making mistakes.

To live fully and take action in life, you must be able to feel **the inner spirit, soul, and self in its perfect goodness inside, and be willing to dive into life and make missteps.** And you just know if you "mess up" you will be accountable and learn from your missteps, so there's no fear. Mistakes are allowed and normal! There is no *guilt or beating yourself up*, just "healthy guilt" or accountability.

Forgiveness is an Act of Courage, and so is accountability. It means you are responsible for your actions and can make mistakes. **This is the only mentality that can move you forward from victimhood and helplessness.**

Once you forgive yourself for your mistakes, you can choose to make amends to help you move through any "healthy guilt" or accountability. Self-rejection is over, and self-acceptance begins.

This is not easy, but it is the most important thing you can do for yourself. As I write this, I realize, of course, that I have made so many mistakes and missteps of my own. I've tried to own them and remedy them where I can within my limits and without being too hard on myself.

That's all we can do, really.

Be kind to ourselves as we continue to learn.

I know that *everything* is forgivable. I don't need another person to tell me what is forgivable or when it is or what punishment they think I "deserve"—because that would be giving them control of my inner peace.

Forgiving Others

ONCE WE START BEING KIND, compassionate, understanding, and forgiving to ourselves, it becomes easy and natural to offer this to others.

We begin to realize that people are just doing their best and doing what they can.

But we cannot forgive others before we are ready. We may be in a place where we feel there is no justice.

If you are in this kind of place, have compassion for yourself during this period. **Do not pressure yourself to forgive someone**; there needs to be *space* for the anger and pain you are experiencing.

The emotions need to be felt. You are the only one who knows what you went through. You are the only one who felt your feelings. You are the only one who understands the pain.

So, allow them all to be felt.

You may be hoping and waiting for the other person to understand what they did and how hurt you are, but this might not be possible. Hopefully, a friend or therapist can listen and offer space for you to feel all your feelings and validate them.

Often, we just need a gentle hand and the presence of another person to allow us to cry in peace. This is a gift another person can offer us (or we can offer to another), one that is more valuable than the millions of dollars we might win in a lottery.

If you are still stuck and angry, you may need to set more boundaries before you can forgive, especially if the other person is still not respecting these.

Or perhaps, if you still see the person who hurt you, their energy might still be affecting you. Maybe you need some distance before you can process the pain. This might help give you the needed space for healing until... one day... you decide it's time to *stop your suffering*. You can have compassion for yourself and decide that you don't want to suffer and go against yourself and your joy anymore!

For this, you can find or create a mantra to repeat. This was mine:

I'm ready to heal.
I'm ready to stop my suffering.
I'm ready to forgive.

Repeat your mantra, and your body will follow your decision to heal.

Forgiveness is an act of self-love in order to stop our own suffering. Eventually, we need to let go of the anger, the pain, and the hurt.

You can stop putting your attention on the hurtful action and instead, place it on processing the sadness, pain, and anger you feel over the event. When you do this, you shift your focus to yourself instead! Your focus is on healing. This is a powerful act of self-love.

Forgiveness is not giving up. It is not agreeing that the "bad" behavior or mistake was okay.

It's just saying,

> "I matter more. My healing matters more than showing you or the world that this behavior was wrong. It means I'm going to lick my wounds instead of standing out there, letting myself bleed, and continuing to object to what you did at my expense.
>
> Once I'm healed, then maybe I will take up a cause to help you and the world deal with this behavior. But not now. Me first; NOW!
>
> I'm not helpless and giving up. I love myself enough to take care of myself in a way that you did not do because I'm more important than you think I am. And I will honor my worth enough to help myself and get help if I need it."

The "I'm ready to stop my suffering" is an important part because it is acknowledging that *you* are able to start and stop your suffering.

You, and only you, have this power.

Wanting Justice

LET'S SAY YOU STILL FEEL stuck in thinking you want justice or revenge even after setting boundaries, taking space, and practising forgiveness and compassion. If that's the case, consider this: If you want justice, then why are you not insisting on the justice of **the whole picture**—rather than just focusing on this incident?

If we really believe in "justice," then I suppose we should also fix the injustices the other person experienced in their life. Why just focus on the event you were involved in? Why not fix the whole thing? **Isn't that more "just"**?

Practice: See everyone that hurt you as a child who was abandoned, doesn't trust, can't communicate, can't open up, is wounded, etc. Only from this view can we truly examine what others "deserve."

Hurt people hurt people.

Sadness

IT'S PART OF BEING HUMAN to feel sadness. The idea that life is supposed to be happy and not *include* sadness or grief is illusory. It is being **in denial and avoiding the natural human experience.**

In daily life, we can often be so busy that we bury or ignore these emotions! When this happens, our emotions can cause harmful effects and start to show up in indirect ways. **Our resistance to releasing them makes them stay with us for longer; otherwise, they will have a shorter life.**

Honor your humanity; the sadness can guide you and might even have a richness to offer you on how to move along on your path. Instead of binge-watching TV, grabbing another drink, or working out to the point of exhaustion, all to avoid coming to terms with how you feel, give yourself permission to cry and honor your pain instead. It is what makes you human.

Allow it.
Feel it.
Grieve.

Just don't abandon yourself.

It's unfortunate that many of us have not received and still don't receive hugs or the magic touch of another human being during difficult times...

In these moments, know that the magic touch of your own hand caressing your forehead or face can release a cascade of much needed tears. To help bring about this self-compassion and heal your nervous system, breathe. Then, while lying in bed in desperation and misery, use your own hand to softly touch your cheek in understanding and care. Allow the release of your tears **and be understanding of yourself for all you went through.**

Have compassion for yourself. Honor your experience. It's true. It's real.

We are often looking for *others* to take care of us or rescue us when we have so many tools available at every moment!

We can also sit in silent meditation, allowing the sad feelings to come out, become visible, and be released. This does not devalue the need or magic of having others there to support us. Rather, these self-love abilities are sometimes all we have, and they're actually a lot!

"Everything in the universe is within you.
Ask all from yourself." – Rumi

A Loving Touch

THERE ARE TIMES WE NEED the physical touch of loving hands. As I shared, sometimes this can be through your own magical touch. You can caress your own face with understanding and compassion. Or you can touch your own heart and send universal energy from your hands to your heart when you are heartbroken.

Some people resist this idea... Why? Is there shame attached to touching your *own* body in love, compassion, comfort, or pleasure? Remember, shame is something that others put on you.

Does it make sense for you to not be "allowed" to touch your own body?

This does not remove what we all know; that being touched in the right way by another person can also have wonderful healing potential. Affection from parents, partners, and friends is one of the main needs we have as humans. After all, the human touch has a human touch!

The hands are the extension
of the heart.

Sound

As we start to feel everything, sound frequency can move and guide us beyond reason! So, experiment with listening to sound of any kind, and allow your body to feel and heal. Allow your body to move and dance. Allow your body to shake and tremble. Allow yourself to listen to a song and cry. Listen and *allow* the sound to play on your heartstrings. Release control.

Just listen and
be moved.

One of my greatest hopes has already come to be for both of my children. They both feel and love music, and this gives me great peace and joy in ways I cannot clearly explain. I am just so glad they have access to this medicine.

Loneliness

LONELINESS IS PART OF THE journey. It is necessary to be alone to really know oneself, and during the process of knowing the self, there may be a lot of loneliness.

Those who felt emotionally abandoned or unsupported as children suffer painful, long-lasting effects as adults. What may help here is inner-child work.

Draw yourself or imagine yourself as the child (or adult, for those who felt this as adults) being abandoned, and then allow another "adult" part of you or a higher self to offer care or safety to this part.

In your hardest moments, you can learn to be there for yourself. **Don't abandon yourself.** Accept your feelings and take care of yourself as well as you can.

Support yourself!

You might also slowly start to see that *life supports you.* We actually cannot be abandoned by life, only by our thinking heads! The universe won't desert you. The universe wants you to live and do your purpose or "job."

Remember, *you are made of love and able to love.* Therefore, your life has purpose and meaning. But if you keep your walls up, stay purely in your Calculator head, and lack self-acceptance, you cannot love. You are closed up and disconnected from yourself. Love happens when you open and uncover your *true nature.*

"Your task is not to seek for love, but merely to seek and find all the barriers within yourself that you have built against it."
– Rumi

When we feel loneliness, we are often feeling a longing for *real connection*. But connection does not come from needing someone to fill our inner feeling of not being "good enough."

In fact, sometimes we might think we are "connected," but really, we are just "attached." For example, we might be attached at the hip with a partner.

Attachment: If you are "attached" you have a *goal*—to receive something or manipulate someone so they can fill a void. You expect them to behave a certain way to make you happy instead of being responsible for your own happiness. You might declare yourself as selfless and generous, but actually, deep down, you are manipulating them toward some end goal or agenda. It's a form of control. We attach using our Calculator heads, not our hearts.

Connection: We connect through the heart. Love is a natural state of kindness and support. It doesn't want anything.

Healthy relating is being *true* and allowing the other person to be *true*. This is connection. If you hide who you are and your emotions from another person to pretend you are strong and not vulnerable, you cannot connect. Connection happens by showing, trusting, and experiencing each other.

Some relationships (the unhealthy ones) do not allow for honesty, and some people may make it "against the rules" to say what you feel, think or need. This commonly occurs in families with addiction and a host of other issues. This is *not* healthy relating. When a person is "forbidden" or otherwise unable to express what they feel (without being aggressive, that is), there is domination and inequality, not a relationship.

Relationships are also unhealthy if one of the parties is un-empathetic and judgmental; it is a setup for heartache. We can be very lonely in these types of relationships.

So as a start, ask yourself, "What is *missing in me* that I think I can get from someone else?"

Can you get "it" from inside?

Is it even possible to get it from outside of yourself? If you live your life controlled by that need for another person to make you feel lovable, you will experience neediness that can *never* be filled. This need will end up controlling you, and you will not be accountable or responsible for your life.

Instead, start spending time **in your own heart.** At first, this might be difficult. Once we begin opening, it can be a slow and painful process. You may feel deep sadness and a disconnect from others. In my opinion, this is one reason people avoid going to the heart.

But if you *do* go there, eventually, with the opening of your own heart, you can start to **feel all your emotions and feel for yourself.**

Eventually, you might come to see and feel that Y♥U are a completely deserving human. And as you find your true nature and start coming out from hiding, you can start to do things that **feel right deep within**. And with time, you can encourage others around you to feel, be vulnerable, and connect on a deeper, more respectful level.

Believe in life and your place in it.

"Out of suffering have emerged the strongest souls; the most massive characters are seared with scars." – Khalil Gibran

Suffering, Surrendering, and Softening

SOMETIMES, IT TAKES DEEP SUFFERING or a dark moment for us to realize that we cannot control everything. In that darkness, there is a surrendering to life. We pray to anything or anyone. And we come to realize there is so much beyond our control.

You may find yourself in such a place where you feel you are in the dark, and you are looking to the outside to shine some light on you or to tell you that you are "beautiful," "deserve better," or are "pure love inside."

What if I were to tell you that you are beautiful, deserving, and pure love already? Well, I can say this... but *I cannot make you see* the Truth.

To feel this Truth *yourself*, you do not need to *do* anything. You just have to get out of the way. In other words, stop covering up who you are, your beauty and Truth. Stop *interfering* with your natural processes of resting, needing space, sitting in silence, allowing your feelings, and following your path.

You need to rest and have space and time alone, to be just like the caterpillar that cocoons and rests,—in what is sometimes a painful process—to transform into a butterfly. In this dark space, a softening can occur—followed by a natural rebirth.

Trust the process.

> *"You have to keep breaking your heart until it opens."* — Rumi

Mantras from Within

DURING DIFFICULTIES, MANY "POSITIVE" AFFIRMATIONS can actually be counterproductive. They put pressure on you, and there is also a discord between what you are *saying* and what you might be *feeling*.

However, at times, mantras or affirmations can be very useful. Sometimes we are in a place of suffering, and yet, at the same time, **there is a small part of us that sees another possibility**. It's a possibility that does not have space and is not yet developed.

For example, let's say a person feels they are defective inside... but there is *also* a little part of them that feels and knows this is not true. Or they are suffering in resentment, and yet there is a piece of them that knows it is *their* job to get out of this.

We can create mantras that come from *within*—not from the outside. The ones we create from within have innate power. Of course, we can also choose and recite existing mantras and chants that feel right for us.

These mantras need repetition to grow, develop, and combat intrusive thoughts. Reciting these mantras in your head whenever a non-helpful thought comes in can be very powerful.

So, a mantra can be like a *true* choice that you are feeding.

But mantras should not be used to replace the necessity of feeling your feelings, of experiencing pain, or as a way of numbing yourself. These feelings need to be felt.

There are times, however, when we know we have felt our feelings enough, and they are no longer serving us. Maybe our mind is spinning or ruminating after we have felt our feelings, set our boundaries, and done all we needed to do. It's just pesky thoughts now that are on repeat mode because they were around for such a long time. You can try to override them with a mantra from the body or a favourite chant.

Ask your *deep self* for a mantra that can serve you, that you believe on some level, even if it's tiny right now. Maybe try, "I'm allowed to take care of myself." Or choose an existing one that feels right for you right now. These can counter untrue or unhelpful thoughts.

The Truth will slowly crowd out untrue thoughts, simply because it carries the power of Truth, and our bodies know it to be so.

Why Asking for Help and Support Is a Power Move

ASKING FOR HELP MEANS YOU matter.

IT MEANS you don't want to be rescued but instead, supported in your process.

IT MEANS you want to get stabilized so you will be able to support others when you can and when they need it.

IT MEANS acknowledging that life is difficult, and we need each other.

IT MEANS we are all the same, and we will all get destabilized and need support at one time or another.

IT MAKES us all equal.

IT MEANS you do not demean or look down upon weakness, vulnerability, and suffering, but that you respect their place.

IT MEANS you do not feel shame about your feelings but are able to feel self-compassion. And therefore, you do not shame others for their difficulties.

IT MEANS you are human.

Ask for support from the universe, earth, your neighbor, anyone you trust enough to do so. And if you refuse to ask for help, then ask yourself:

"Why not?"

Being Open to Receive

BEING OPEN TO RECEIVING MIGHT sound obvious. You might laugh and think, "Yes, I'm open to getting gifts," but it's really not that simple. Truly being open to receiving has an undertone... a feeling that **you are deserving.** When this is the case, your cells are literally open.

Let's just say I am here to give you a piece of bread, and as I try to give it to you, your fists tense and clench... Can you receive the gift? And, if I were to try to give you a hug, could your body and heart receive it? What about my help or a kind word? If your answer is no, why not? Do you feel you do not deserve it?

Are you open to receiving the sun's rays? Can you receive compassion from yourself? Can you receive without calculating the "exchange" or what you will now owe?

Just because you are deserving?

If your answer is "no," then think back. When did you start believing that you are *undeserving* of receiving help, compliments, information from the universe, or intuition? Look deeply for the Truth.

Just because someone did something unkind to you at some point in your life, it does not mean you were or are "bad" or that their view of you was "correct." It does not mean you don't deserve good things to come your way!

Expanding
Your Being

What Is Ego?

To STUDY THE QUESTION OF ego, let's first look at how you sit, stand, and walk—your posture.

Are you walking around with your head high **above** others, calculating and acting as if some people are *beneath* you for whatever reason? Maybe you think they are not as smart as you, not of the same race, not as rich, or not as good-looking.

Or are you walking around with your head low and **below** others, calculating and acting as if some people are *above* you for whatever reason? Maybe you think other people are smarter than you, of a "better" race or ethnicity, wealthier, or better-looking?

These are two sides of the same coin. Both come from the thinking Calculator and not from **the Truth, which lies in the tenderness of our hearts.**

All the ego stuff, both above and below, is formed as a reaction to childhood rejection, ingrained childhood superiority complexes, or other difficulties and traumas. It is the result of trying to cope with the fears and hurts including that of not being seen and listened to as every human deserves. And it will stay around until we know and understand ourselves deeply.

This ego, which creates the idea that you are superior or inferior to others, separates *you* and *me* from the *true you* and *true me*. This prevents us from truly connecting. This "analytical and comparing energy" (energy in the head) creates stories and drives us further and further from the Truth and reality.

But instead of being stuck in this Calculator, we can look to our body and our emotions to guide us back to our true selves **if we just listen to and feel them instead of avoiding them.**

And we can use our curiosity to question the concepts of superiority and inferiority and instead look for the Truth within.

Our Sameness

ULTIMATELY, ANY PHILOSOPHY, RELIGION, OR belief which makes a person superior or inferior to another is missing the point.

The point is that we are all *souls* (energy, spirits, beings) living different experiences, all of which we can understand and have compassion for—no matter what.

If we spent our entire lifetime listening without judgement to one person, we could understand everything about them, everything they do, and everything they feel. But of course, we cannot do that all day long with every person.

We can, however, spend the time understanding *ourselves*! And once we are at a place where we understand ourselves, our pain, our reactions, and our everything, **we no longer judge ourselves.** Because we understand.

When we really understand ourselves, there's no way to be critical because **it all makes sense.** We accept everything about ourselves and start to act from this wisdom with others. We understand our sameness and equality. **No one is superior.**

"I speak to everyone in the same way, whether [they are] the garbage man or the president of the university." – Albert Einstein

Unique Flower

ALL SUPERIORITY AND INFERIORITY COMPLEXES are false and can lead to years of being on a confusing and painful path. Superiority and inferiority can appear in unexpected and subtle ways. Even *pitying* someone has a *superior* quality to it.

Just feel what I mean by that. How might it make you feel superior when you are pitying someone else?

It's the same with admiration. How does admiring someone in an unhealthy way make you feel? Are they *superior* to you?

Spend some time noticing your feelings when you are with someone and observing how often there is a tone (whether yours or theirs) of "I'm better than you" or "I'm worse than you." This is an undertone of calculating and comparing each other, which leads to disconnection.

Now, take a piece of paper and draw a picture of yourself and a few other people you know. Anyone. Now add a picture or image of Mother Teresa, Buddha, or whomever you believe to have a loving nature, and really, really look at this picture.

Will the figure in the picture be comparing and "ranking" you and everyone you drew? Why or why not?

When you looked at this picture, did you start to think that Buddha, Mother Teresa, or another person with a loving nature was **better** than you?

If so, you have a mistaken understanding of YOU!

Can you imagine instead that each and every one of us has a spirit, a soul, a life, a being? There are no leaders and no followers.

Each person is absolutely meant to be here and is absolutely perfect, and unique at the same time.

Your **essence** is your unique perfume. Your essence is the deeper you. It's what you are looking for, searching up, down, and everywhere for. But it's right here. *You* are right here!

Your essence never changes. Think back to when you were seven years old and then to when you were fifteen years old. Your essence was the same back then as it is now. You might make different choices and have different behaviors and experiences. But your essence is the same.

All your behaviors and actions are *not* your essence. Your job, marriages, successes, titles, and mistakes are *not* your essence. Your essence is the *true you*.

I take a moment to think of my daughter, her essence, which I can almost smell like a flower. I close my eyes and inhale. I smile as I sense her deep beauty, strength, wisdom, and goodness in my heart.

I take a moment and think of my son. I can feel his essence from miles away. I close my eyes and inhale. I smile as I sense his deep Courage, sensitivity, wisdom, and goodness in my heart.

My heart opens feeling them. Such gifts. Thank you both for being my guides.

Have you ever tried to sense someone's essence? Take a moment to try to experience this with the next person you speak with. Can you speak to their essence?

Can you feel your *own* essence, rest in it and just BE?

What Is Being?

THERE IS NOTHING YOU NEED to *do* to be human and have innate value.

Just sit and
be you.

Breathe,

listen, and

feel.

Kindergarten Heart

SOME PEOPLE WORRY THAT IF we don't have all the rules, controls, punishments, shame, and guilt from various sources in place, then people will be selfish, inconsiderate, and hurtful. They believe that rules based on guilt, punishment, and shame are necessary to control our *evil* nature.

I don't believe it! Our nature is good!

We don't need outside guilt, rules, and control. In fact, these likely created all the issues we have inside!

What better way to control and confuse and disempower people than by telling them they are innately *flawed, bad,* or *evil,* so they accept rules established to control them. We internalize shame and guilt and spend our entire life trying to "fix" ourselves!

What better way to control someone than by telling them, directly or indirectly, not to trust or express their innate wisdom?

What better way to control someone than by telling them they are only a good person *if* they listen to their rules?

You don't have to believe these stories. You can sense and trust in your own true good nature.

But don't mix up this good nature with your *behavior.* Your **inside essence is pure goodness**—but it's also true your behaviors might not be good for you or hurtful to others. That's why we need to look within and be honest with ourselves.

The problem is that if you always doubt or are insecure about your inside goodness, you cannot *see* your behavior, accept your mistakes, learn and be accountable, since this will feel like it diminishes you. You would "lose points" on the ranking scale you have created for yourself.

If, however, you are secure and *know your goodness*, then you can see anything!

Your behavioral mistakes do not affect you deeply, for you know everything is a learning or growing experience. So, if someone expresses to you that they feel something is "negative" or hurtful in your behavior, you are open to hearing their view and then deciding what you'd like to do. You are able to do this because you are open to looking and learning, since nothing you do touches upon your inner sanctity.

Inside you are still
and at peace.

Loving Eyes

ON YOUR PATH, YOU WILL encounter many people who ignore you, and it might be painful, at least until you feel more secure and stable.

But I'd like to explain what I mean by "ignoring."

They might speak to you or look at you, but they can be ignoring your essence or looking *through you*. This is because they do not see themselves as "divine." They are looking at you using the Calculator. Their eyes are cold. They might be looking at you only to get something.

```
It's dehumanizing. We are not robots.
It's dehumanizing to look at people as if they
do not exist.
It's dehumanizing to look at people like they
are just pieces of meat or objects to serve
someone's own needs.
It's dehumanizing to rank the big CEO as more
"valuable" than the kind person at the post of-
fice, thus equating human worth with money.
That is demeaning to all of us!
```

Unfortunately, ignoring the essence of another is fairly common. When others are not looking at you and seeing your essence, then DO NOT believe what you see in their eyes, in that mirror.

You will know when you are looked at with the "right" or loving eyes. Those eyes might only be *your own*, or you might be lucky enough to encounter a person who will look at your essence correctly.

If you don't have such an encounter with someone else, it's not because your essence does not exist or there is something wrong with you. It's that most people are stuck in their Calculator heads and have not seen and felt their *own* hearts deep within—because, as humans, we *lose sight* when we are thinking instead of sensing and feeling. The eyes are the window of the soul, the saying goes—but they are not yet able to see yours.

In moments you feel present, try looking at yourself or others in the eyes with acceptance instead of judgment. Try to see them *with your heart.*

Try listening to others and having compassion for their pain. Look at people at the same eye level when sitting in front of them. No one needs to look up or down at anyone during communication.

> "Shut your eyes so the heart may become your eye, and with that vision, look upon another world." – Rumi

The Only "Problems"
You Need to Solve

FEELING ALLOWED TO BE YOU, liking yourself, loving yourself, and feeling your innate goodness and essence are the only "problems" you need to "solve" during your lifetime.

These are no small problems, as they guide your every move—what you buy, how you speak with people, what you choose in life, and so forth.

So don't worry so much about what car to buy or what shirt to wear. Solve those "problems" instead, and everything else will fall into place!

As a parent, what do I want for my kids when they "grow up"? I simply wish for them to figure out how to love, trust, and follow themselves.

It takes a lot of self-love and Courage to live with this deep sense of worthiness no matter what the world around you says. But it's certainly possible to do so and it is actually quite relaxing.

Loving Yourself as Your Number One "Goal"

SOMEONE ONCE TOLD ME, AFTER an incident where I set boundaries, that, according to them, I "caused a drama."

"Your most important goal in your life *should be* the relationship with the family," I was told.

"No," I answered. "My most important goal is my relationship with myself." Because my "goal" was to learn how I could be:

- More peaceful
- Less controlling
- More loving and compassionate
- Less tolerant of abusive behavior
- A better listener to myself and others
- More confident to act from my own essence.

Is it even possible to love another person before you love yourself? I doubt it. And if one does, then it wouldn't be in a healthy way.

Love and joy are experienced on the inside—and we **cannot get them from someone else.** They arise from an internal experience, from the permission to **be you 24/7,** and only you can choose to do this.

Following your Truth also helps the whole world, whether you understand exactly in what way or not. When you follow your Truth, you stop all kinds of behaviors that are rooted in insecurity about who you are or your value.

Healed people heal people.

The concept of "love your brothers, sisters, neighbors, or enemies" makes no sense if one does not first love the *self*. It is impossible to love another person in a true sense if you do not love and accept your own self.

So, we should all be encouraged to love our *true selves*. To all politicians, peace workers, parents, and others:

Please turn your efforts towards yourselves, and you will be more helpful to our world.

Things like martyrdom and sacrifice are not evidence of love, as we have been taught. They are just signs of a lack of self-love and, therefore, proof that you do not genuinely love the other person. You are "getting something" from this martyrdom, and that is why you are doing it.

Learn to be **kind to yourself and do not let guilt get in the way.** It's amazing how many things we can feel guilty about. We can feel guilty about feeling joy instead of being "productive." We can even feel guilty if we take time to rest or grieve. Nonsense!

Be kind to yourself, and you will *naturally* become kinder to others and insist on kindness within your personal relationships.

That's why *it all starts with self* and grows from there.

Make loving yourself your number one job!

No More People-Pleasing

WE ARE OFTEN DISHONEST WITH ourselves and others because the Truth can be painful, and being honest can sometimes have difficult consequences. Being honest takes great Courage.

Choose it anyway!

Ask yourself, "Do I spend my life doing 'nice' things for others and trying to make them happy?" If so, what is the source of this?

Are you doing this just to be liked? Are you doing this to not "rock the boat"? Why are you trying to make people happy? Do you feel like you need them to like you?

People-pleasing isn't "loving" people. These actions likely stem from you wanting to convince others that **you are good and to get their positive feedback.**

But can you see how this will not work? All of us grow up with others praising and criticizing us. But no matter how "good" anyone ever thinks you are, no matter how much you give to charity or how much of your time you volunteer, the other person (who is *outside* you) is now "holding the cards," so to speak, on deciding whether you are "good" or "bad" at any given moment!

The outside world is controlling you completely, and this will continue no matter what you do **until you see the Truth of your goodness and know that your essence is pure** no matter what has happened in the past.

You are goodness even if you sit on the floor all day and do nothing. Your deep self is good and deserves to be treated with kindness.

So instead of living with the constant worry of, "What if they get mad at me?" or, "What if they think this or that?" just **be you** whether you are appreciated or not. Whether they are pleased or not.

Yes, some of your relationships may get affected because of this, and you may lose some of the people in your life, but it only proves those were very weak relationships and were not based on Truth and love anyway.

When you live life only for other people's approval and go against yourself, or if you always cave to outer pressure, you are abandoning yourself. You are abandoning your inner child and sacrificing yourself for others.

Do not abandon yourself.

If you were "trained" not to disappoint others and faced serious repercussions if you did, know that you don't have to remain in that mode anymore. You don't have to walk around making others happy, even pleasing your children so they like you. You have a choice!

You can stop being a people pleaser!

Truly Helping

ANOTHER DIFFICULT QUESTION TO ASK yourself and to be honest about is your "helping" habits. When you are helping another out, are you actually trying to help the other person or are you being helpful because you are just trying to feel better about yourself? Do you think, "I am a better person because I helped out"?

There is a difference between caretaking and caregiving.

Care*taking* is a hallmark of codependency and is rooted in insecurity and a need to be in control. (I am not talking about employed caretakers.) The word "take" is included in caretaking because we take and get something out of the caring. For example, feeling useful or worthy. A care*taker* feels needed and superior to the other person, and at the same time, is assured their partner won't leave them because the partner always needs them to take care of them. This kind of helping turns into or feels like control. Caretakers take from the recipient or give with strings attached.

Care*giving*, on the other hand, is an expression of kindness and love. Caregiving honors another person. Care*giving* is giving freely. It is not so much about the specific action of helping but about our own *intention* and how we feel inside. There are no strings attached.

This, as usual, is so hard to see and to be honest about! We all like to see ourselves as kind, generous, and helpful, versus acknowledging the fact that we have issues with self-worth. Therefore, we try to get it anywhere we can, even by caretaking.

It can also be hard to see if our actions are *actually helping* another or "enabling" them to continue their unhealthy behavior. Sometimes a person might be weakening others so that they can feel useful, powerful, and worthy themselves. This can, of course, happen subconsciously; we don't even realize it! We might be "saving" someone and "helping" them when they have an addiction, for example. And our actions might actually enable the other person to continue their addiction longer instead of getting help.

Sometimes you can be the best helper by "dropping" a person, so they understand their behavior is not okay. That feedback can turn out to be helpful for them!

And in the case where you are the person being "helped," ask yourself whether the other person is *actually* helping you. Someone can give you advice to feel superior. They might help you simply because they are addicted to feeling needed and receiving gratitude. Their "helping" might weaken you because they keep "saving you" and giving you the message that **you can't do it without them.** This person is not helping you. A way to find clarity about your relationship with them is to ask yourself: "Do I feel **stronger** or **weaker** after interacting with them?"

So, the next time you think of offering anyone help, once again, remember that your number one job is to love yourself. Then your helping someone is more likely to be coming from the right place, and that is what matters. Your actions and words will be intuitively "right" at the moment. There is no recipe. The right intention and intuition will deal with this. There are no rules—just trust your natural flow.

Today, for example, I might be most helpful to the world by writing these words, or perhaps most helpful to my family by sitting and finding my own peace.

Keeping the Peace

"KEEPING THE PEACE" IS A funny phrase. What peace? Whose peace?

I once experienced an incident where someone behaved in a way that I felt was verbally hostile and disrespectful towards me during an event, which led me to setting boundaries around their behavior. Others requested that I "just relax" and "let it go" for the sake of "keeping the peace."

How does tolerating such behavior create peace in the world?

Peace begins with **self-love**, followed by **actions that originate from self-love**—without putting another person down. If one truly has self-love, they are incapable of putting down another person, since they understand their own internal essence and thus, that of the other.

Peace does not mean allowing abuse or other behavior to hurt us. Peace does not mean just sitting there and allowing any behavior to continue.

By trying to keep the peace outside, we *destroy the peace inside*. Is that helpful to the world?

The day after the incident—which was chaotic and not peaceful on the outside—I woke up exhausted, drained, sad, and needing support from a friend.

But I also had no anxiety, nor did I second-guess myself.

Please keep the peace... *inside*.

Who's Responsible?

SOME OF US TAKE RESPONSIBILITY for others' actions and allow ourselves to be treated as punching bags or scapegoats. Someone might tell you, "You made me mad," or "You made me do this." Love is not about taking abuse or taking responsibility for other people's behavior.

Knowing this, I try not to accept responsibility for actions that were not mine. But this is hard, for the other person might not agree they are accountable.

But, as before, other people's choices are not in our control. What we *can do* is not to accept responsibility for things we *didn't do*.

In these situations, continue to act in accordance with *your* Truth—you are responsible for your own actions, thoughts, and feelings, **and that's it**. You can try to explain to a person that their behavior is hurting you, but they might not see it from your perspective and might keep behaving the same way. If this happens, release the control, and trust that the universe will take care of this in due time.

You cannot control their thoughts and feelings, so take full control and accountability for *your part* and *your life*—make sure you are well and move on.

Opening and Expanding

WHAT OPENS OR CLOSES YOU up? You can look at whether your chest opens or closes around certain people, during different activities, and in any particular environment.

What lifts you up or pushes you down? Notice what or who makes your eyes gaze lower.

Always ask yourself, "Does this [person, place, thing] make me stronger or weaker?"

The situation or person that weakens you is the very one you need to stand up to. Whether it's a person or situation, you may need to walk away and take your power back from where you gave it.

You will need to stand up to anyone who has ever tried to put you down.

You can stand up to them in your room, in your imagination, or in person (all the while respecting that the other person is a human being and not lashing out at them).

You can stand up to anyone who did not recognize your glorious humanity, who did not recognize that you have feelings, an inner compass, and that you have a right to be here and to be YOU.

Team Rise

IN A WORLD WHERE EVERYONE around you, even your own thoughts, might be putting you down, maintaining self-compassion is a *refusal to be hard on yourself* and to continue on that trajectory.

It is a decision to stop beating yourself up, to start understanding everything about yourself, and to **help yourself.**

This simple act, though it might look messy, tearful, and chaotic, is a **choice to rise up.** That's why self-compassion is an **Act of Courage!** It comes from your inner fire, which we all have (although sometimes we discover it only after hitting rock bottom).

You are on the path of: "I exist, and rightfully so. Let me see what's going on with me and help myself, instead of blaming myself, hurting myself, and belittling myself, as so many people do."

It's a decision to be on **Team Rise** (and to stand up to the "bullying" by the Calculator head and others) versus being a part of **Team Push Down** (criticizing, putting down, and disempowering).

Eventually, once the battle is over (and by the way, no one has to be harmed during this battle since it is basically an internal battle) and you have risen, **you can sit in clarity, power, and strength and be on everyone else's Team Rise!**

You will now be the cheerleader instead of the person who weakens people. And of course, this would not be the cheering on of what *you* believe to be success and perpetuating outer validation, but rather, cheering people on to trust their inner compass and to be empowered. That's what will *actually* help!

Your Best Friend

WHO IS YOUR BEST FRIEND? Are you your own best friend? The one who always understands you and never abandons you?

The Truth is that you are actually the only one who can always understand yourself because you know yourself best.

Live your Truth by being your own best friend and constantly asking yourself, "What's my Truth if I'm honest with myself?"

Strive to be a good friend to yourself first, instead of striving to making outside people happy.

Listening to Yourself

Do you actually listen to yourself, or do you just judge yourself? Do you give yourself the time and space to feel and listen?

To listen to ourselves, we need to develop an inner silence (silencing the judging) and look deeper within into the part of ourselves that *knows,* so we can make choices and take actions aligned with this knowing.

But if you're in the habit of not listening to yourself, and you just do what a "good person" is "supposed" to do, it will take a lot of Courage to start trusting your inner voice. You will need Courage to be honest about what you feel and the choices you want to make, instead of focusing on whether you will be disappointing other people.

Once you are used to listening and respecting this inner voice, you will become less tolerant of relationships where people undermine or criticize you or your choices.

Your new "way" might even be
contagious and encourage others to
listen to their own inner voices!

Fear Is Contagious,
But So Is Courage

COURAGE DOES NOT HAVE TO be a heroic event. Courage can be a small act, maybe just getting out of bed on a particular day.

If you form a Courage Group with others after reading this book, or if you just want to share this idea with a friend, go ahead and share some stories where you felt courageous with each other, so you can sense and feel the energy of Courage.

Courage is contagious!

Stories are powerful to humans and we can en*Courage* each other by sharing our stories.

Courage is our **knowing power in motion.** When we act with Courage, it means we **know** something inside and might need to trust the unknown when we act in accordance with this inner knowing. Even though the unknown doesn't necessarily mean "bad," Courage often takes some trust and a leap of faith.

Support those who choose to be courageous instead of questioning, doubting, or undermining them. Give support to those who trust their Truth and are moving forward on their path, even if that path is different than yours.

Are you ready to feel a moment of Courage?

It does not have to be a heroic or larger-than-life act. It can simply be the way you sit quietly in a room, exuding your

Courage in *being you*—which is not an easy feat by any means! Everyone in your presence (and perhaps even beyond) will feel this energy.

Living courageously will be contagious! The people around you will feel your energy and perhaps take this on for themselves.

Step 1: Live in Courage no matter what and let go of any outcome.

Step 2: Repeat step 1.

Pride and Confidence

Others often tell us what we *should* feel proud of:

"You should be proud of yourself for getting that A."
"You should be proud of yourself for scoring the winning goal!"
"You should feel proud of your child for achieving something."
"You should feel proud of yourself for looking so good."

Well, my proudest moments have often been when I expressed myself and set boundaries in difficult situations. At times it was in the midst of conflict but I managed to stand up for myself. And even though this sometimes brought me to tears and distress at the time, this is also where I felt like patting myself on the back, even though no one else thought I *should* feel proud of myself.

This is an example of healthy pride and not ego. **Healthy pride is feeling good about yourself** versus feeling superior or comparing yourself to others. It's feeling good about something *from your interior* without all the comparing.

Try allowing yourself to feel healthy pride as a step to pulling yourself out of an old state of shame. You might have to overcome some old fears to do this. For example, maybe you're afraid that people will judge you or question you about this change. Be patient with yourself as you build this confidence slowly.

What can you feel proud of today?

- Maybe you managed to write a journal entry today.
- Maybe you took a shower and cared for yourself.
- Maybe you simply got out of bed and got dressed to face another day even while you are going through a difficult time.

Allow yourself to feel healthy pride for still being alive and *not giving up.* That's not an easy thing to do during difficult times!

Like many other emotions, healthy pride will show in your posture. Do you walk around slumped (feeling inferior)? Is your nose up in a dominant posture (feeling superior)? Or does your posture simply reflect healthy pride in the person you truly are, **radiating kindness, equality, compassion, self-confidence, and Courage?**

Even if you haven't reached a place of healthy pride yet, try to stand tall anyway. No matter your actual height. No matter how others look at you.

This feeling and posture positively affects your breathing and allows you to draw the energy from the earth up to the crown of your head. This will open your heart and you will feel the strength of your spine.

So, what is true confidence? The word **confide** is at the root: "to place trust or have faith."

There you go! To have self-**confide**nce, you need to trust yourself!

I Matter

WE HAVE ALL HAD MOMENTS where we feel powerless, useless, and insignificant. You might have had thoughts like, "Why do I matter? Little old me? Of what 'use' am I?"

Well, this is how I see things:

Imagine we are all on the same ship called *Life*. And there is a natural and positive direction to this ship. So, just pick up a paddle and matter. **Anyone who feels they do not matter is not paddling... yet.**

Perhaps you thought you had to pull the whole entire ship on your own. That's your ego talking.

Get up, do your work, do your share. **Do You,** whatever that is. It matters!

We are all butterflies with the power of having the butterfly effect. Scientifically, according to chaos theory, this means that even small actions such as a butterfly flapping its wings can have a large consequence. It might even affect the direction of a future tornado!

Your share might be smiling at someone, learning about music, going for a walk in the woods to appreciate the beauty of nature, or whatever else you may choose.

Life matters.
I matter. You matter.
Everything matters.

When you make this connection with yourself and Life, then you are not focused on a personal relationship with anyone. **It is your relationship with yourself and with Life that really matters.** The rest will come naturally.

You are moving around Life "alone." You may be crossing paths with other people, but you are alone to do what you are to do. Whatever that is.

And part of this "doing what you are to do" includes resting, crying, discovering your deep self, and expressing yourself. So, connect with yourself and follow it. Follow what feels right.

Connect with yourself and with Life, and you will not be lonely because you are *with* Life and *with* everyone. You are on the same side as everyone and Life. You are going *with* the flow.

CONNECTION TO YOU

+

CONNECTION TO ALL OF LIFE

———————————————————

=

GOING WITH THE FLOW OF LIFE

What Is Choice?

IF YOU IGNORE YOURSELF AND are controlled by outside forces and only choose what others think you should... **is that really even a choice**?

We can also be controlled by our inner critic, guilt, and shame (which are also **external** elements, since they were put there by others and internalized by us), and again, this is not *actually* choosing.

Once you see this, you can move towards being guided by your inner compass.

We can start to expand our hearts, respect our feelings, and have more clarity. We can now make a choice in any situation.

If *you* are the source of choice, if *you* choose instead of allowing *them* to make your choices, then you are POWERFUL!

And with every choice, you'll learn something else from this teacher and continue along your path.

Power

THE WORD SELF-LOVE MAY SOUND lovey-dovey, but actually, it is very powerful. As you might have started to notice, this book is actually about **POWER**.

Just imagine...

- You don't need approval, thereby limiting all the effects of advertisements, sales, and marketing ploys, which try to convince you that you need their services and products to feel good about yourself. **You cannot be controlled.**
- Imagine you do not want to please anyone. **You cannot be controlled.**
- Imagine you don't fall for manipulation or guilt, and just act from your own center. **You cannot be controlled.**
- Imagine you don't depend on anyone in order to feel like a good person or worthy. **You cannot be controlled.**
- Imagine you make your choices from the inside. **You cannot be controlled.**

If you are practising and learning to listen inside, you will start to ask yourself, "What am I compelled, drawn, and inspired to do?" You are not asking yourself about what you *have to do* according to others, but instead, you are looking at what's coming from the inside. **This is your power!**

Yet, we are somewhat afraid of this power. We know that this is an Act of Courage that others might not appreciate.

Those who are obsessed with controlling others (controlling their outside instead of living from their inside) might not appreciate a person they cannot easily control with guilt, shame, or pressure.

They want to control others because *they* don't feel good inside, connected to others or the Universe. They do not feel powerful themselves.

Many of us have been trained to be afraid of the word "power" or the idea of using our own power, as if doing so is evil or immoral.

But this kind of power is *not finite*. There's no need to compete for it or to grab your part of the power and hoard it. Each person can live in full power. Not power *over* others. But *in their own power*.

Surround yourself with those who have found their own power, who do not try to control you, and who encourage you to live in your power. Soon enough, you will feel *strong enough inside* to encounter anyone and anything and know that you can and will make choices from the inside, no matter what happens.

This, my friend, is inner peace; knowing you have the tools *inside* you at any time. It doesn't mean you won't suffer physically, be sad, or lose people in your life, but you will always know you can sit, feel, make choices, and rebalance your inner self each time.

Self-Love Is Not Selfish

WHEN YOU TAKE CARE OF or follow yourself, people might accuse you of being selfish. They may say this because they no longer have control over you to get you to do what they want.

The irony is, however, that the more self-love you have, the **more love you have for others**! But of course, it's the real kind! Not the people-pleasing kind.

All acts of self-love are "correct." They will lead to "right" things in the world no matter what it looks like in the moment. They are not an act *against* anyone but are an act *for* you. If you do not act with self-love, then you are *against* yourself... and that's why our world is in big trouble.

Once you realize this, you understand why you need to take care of yourself. **Because you matter. Because you have a "mission" here**—even if you don't know exactly what it is yet. When you do, your reason for taking care of yourself becomes *bigger than you*. You take care of yourself because you have a duty to the world.

Your duty can be almost anything. It varies from person to person and across moments of time. It might be to paint, then to feel good, and then to smile at someone. It might be to read for five years before you share a story with a child at the right time.

Do not judge your "mission." Just follow your intuition and trust that it is as it should be. **You are exactly as you should be.**

The only way to heal the world is to heal ourselves. When one person heals, they send out ripples.

Is self-love easy? No. My path there has included many lonely nights, inner crises, so many tears, and rebellion. But I am more at peace now than ever.

Isn't that what you are looking for too? Well, then go ahead. **Pick up your Courage and trust.** Trust that your "rebellion" against what you used to do and allow in your life will lead you to inner peace in the end.

I now trust the wisdom of the Universe and the Truth within me.

You were created with a certain heart and soul by which you are meant to be guided. What people have "done to you" has nothing to do with you. It's not personal.

Life is not against you.

Life is always on your side.

Breathe, Surrender, and Rest in Being

TAKE A BREAK FROM READING this book for a few breaths to rest in Being. After one of your exhales, wait a moment, surrender, and let yourself *be breathed*... Open your heart as your breath rises to the top of your crown so you can meet the universe.

I belong to this earth.

So do you.

I belong here to do my "soul's" work.

So do you.

The earth will hold you, music will soothe you,

and tears will heal you.

Your inner light and fire

will guide you.

Time For Courage

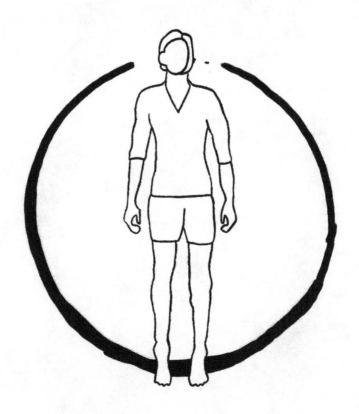

Standing Up After Sitting Down

AFTER SITTING IN MEDITATION WITH yourself, you can now decide to stand up for yourself. Your *true self*. This is particularly hard if you are not used to asserting yourself, and it can take time if you don't have a strong sense of self yet. It's a courageous thing to do, as this might "break" or redefine some relationships and even create outer conflict on your way to inner peace.

Inner work is not just about sitting for hours in meditation; it's about spending time inside so that you can then learn to **make choices aligned with you**.

It's about standing up, being a human being, and expressing your freedom to be who you really are. Don't worry about how it will all play out. Just allow your Courage, love and trust to intertwine.

After all this sitting in your Truth and in meditation with yourself, are you ready to **STAND UP**?

Standing Alone

WE GENERALLY IDENTIFY WITH A group: family, country, sports team... any "clan" out of desperation, fear, and insecurity. We want to try to be part of a "side."

And we are constantly dealing with the fact that people cannot see or understand us, which, in my experience, occurs because they cannot see themselves. **So, you will often need to stand alone in your knowing.** Know your worth when others do not see your value, and understand this is because they do not *know their own*.

You will often need to stand alone when listening to your inner compass and making choices others don't agree with. Try to be strong and deeply rooted like a tree when no one agrees with you except you. **You, and only you, have to be ready to dive into the unknown and to lean into all these new possibilities.**

It is only when we are ready to stand alone that we truly flourish. This is emotional freedom and sovereignty.

The idea is not to stand up for your country, for your football team, or for your school, **but for yourself.** Just be in self-love and see what happens around you.

It will not necessarily be pretty, and that's why it is an act of Courage.

But remember, you are a force of nature!

To some, standing alone might sound like a horrible existence. It's not. When you learn to stand alone, and when this slowly becomes contagious to others with whom you interact, you'll experience a new level of connecting and relating without control because this is what you exude and teach **just by being you.** So, ironically, you will feel *less* alone and much more connected to anyone you encounter!

Imagine all of us as trees. Each tree must stand on its own rooted in Mother Earth. And in the forest, there is no judgment about the branching out that the other trees need to do.

Be a tree.

Identify as a tree.

Response-Ability

A PERSON SITTING IN THEIR POWER is a person who takes responsibility. This means always trying to see our part or how we can make choices in a situation instead of giving all our power away.

You are responsible for your life. You have the ability to make choices.

Response-ability.

If you make a turn in your life's path and then feel you need to make a new turn, then make another choice. You are **in charge!** You have the **ability** to make choices and you have the perfect system inside guiding you. You are not a robot. You exist; you matter. And you are *responsible*.

If we are always pointing fingers and saying something happened "because of someone else," we have wiped out our **power!**

Admitting we have a choice is rehumanizing and nourishes our inner freedom. If we don't think we have any choices, we won't hear our Truth in meditation, since we feel we can't choose anything anyway; the two go hand in hand. Seeing or hearing the Truth is an opportunity to learn and to make another choice instead of feeling *helpless* and unable to choose.

A person who has a habit of *blaming others* can become chronically angry in order to avoid taking responsibility for their life or dealing with their old wounds. Of course, we can always blame, nitpick, and find fault instead of being accountable and making choices, but an empowered person chooses the accountability road. It's not just the "high road"—**it's the powerful and life-respecting road.**

If you know you have the tendency to blame, here's another very odd thing that you might be doing; you might be accusing others *of what you yourself are doing!* I remember I accused someone of being impatient once, only to realize the impatient one was actually me! (This is called projecting.)

So, who do you look to, to solve
your life problems or "rescue" you,
instead of looking in the mirror?

Making Choices

IF YOU ARE STARTING TO feel some Courage and you're ready to use your power of choice, then how can you know what to choose? Where does choice come from?

If you are still stuck in your *thoughts,* you might think there is a "problem" to solve and you are trying to choose the solution. But is there actually a problem or are you, as we've already seen, just avoiding your feelings by going inside your head? Instead, get in the habit of going into your body. Most of our thoughts are about solving insecurity or avoiding feelings. Maybe we are afraid and hurt and still angry, and this needs to be felt. All of it. Once we do this, and practice self-acceptance, many of our thoughts will naturally subside and we can start to open up and see new possibilities.

Other pesky thoughts that also get in the way of using our power of choice arise when we live with a constant attempt to find total certainty, such as: "What will happen if I do this? Should I do this then?" "What if, what if?" If we are busy trying to predict every possible outcome, it is very hard to make **choices** from this space.

The Truth is that the *only* certainty there is, is what is happening right now.

Let me explain. If I am absolutely feeling terrible, that is the Truth. That is certain. And if we stay looking at the Truth of now, we are in the reality of life, and **only in this space can we actually see our power of choice** in the moment and the open windows around us.

We spend a lot of time unable to make decisions by over-analyzing and being insecure about the future, and the outcomes of all of the decisions we could potentially make.

Living in this constant tension of uncertainty and indecisiveness is a "stuck" place to be. Given how life moves, there is no exact certainty and there is no predictability of outcomes.

But it's not as bad as it sounds. There is something very comforting! Even though we cannot predict all the outcomes, because it's impossible, we can make decisions from our core, intuition, compass, and feelings. And soon we learn and see that, **regardless of the outcome, this is a "good" choice!**

This is what sitting in meditation does for me. When I'm confused, hurt, and uncertain, I sit with myself and allow what I feel. Then, I look for what *I feel I should do*. I try to use my gut feeling, my heart, my inner knowing, instead of just my head.

When something just *feels* right, and although I do not know exactly why right then, I try to be comfortable with the *unknown* of it and trust it anyway. **My trust in my compass is stronger than the fear of the unknown. That's where the magic lies!**

The more you do this, the more you can see that we are equipped with a "direction" that we can *sense*. It might be a rocky or painful path, but it can still be right.

So instead of always asking "what if" questions, which brings on the thinking mind, try asking:

"What *feels right* for me right now?"

Getting Out of Your Uncomfortable Zone

WE'VE ALL HEARD THE TERM "comfort zone," but I feel this term isn't well understood. The assumption is that the place we are in is comfortable, but actually, it's not necessarily comfortable at all!

It is just the *known*.

If you stay in a relationship because you're in your comfort zone, then you are comfortable with this relationship because you have an idea in your head of how it will be every day. But what if that same relationship is an abusive one? The relationship might feel "comfortable" to you today because it is familiar. It's what you know, even if it's abusive!

So you keep choosing the familiar.

Now, what if you were to *leave it*? That's going to the **unknown.** Therefore, it's outside the comfort (known) zone and less familiar to you. The Calculator does not like this, since it cannot predict this new scenario.

But what's so good about predictability anyway?

That's what our Calculator head does all day long—tries to follow predictability. But that's a limited way to live. It's stagnant and prevents you from expanding.

Planning vs. the Unknown

WE PLAN AND PLAN TO project the known (our past experience) into the future so that we might have some idea and certainty of the outcome. This makes some sense, of course.

But, in doing things this way, we cannot be creative or feel the right path for ourselves and are limited to only a finite number of possibilities. We disregard the fact that the future is uncertain and cannot be "planned out" in this way.

Mathematically, this planning makes no sense, since the number of factors that can affect our moments and days cannot be calculated. They are too complex. But, as I mentioned, this is not a bad thing. It just means that constant planning based on information from the past is not feasible.

We cannot predict or control it all, and we can't know how everything will play out. All these rigid expectations are pure suffering! Each time something doesn't happen that you expected to happen, you compare your current moment with your expectation and wind up feeling disappointed.

For example, you go on a bike ride and *expect* it all to be great. Halfway though, the chain breaks. If you have rigid expectations, then you spend the next thirty minutes frustrated, **comparing what you expected with what actually happened** because it doesn't match the expectation you rigidly created. You are in your head, miserable and stuck!

But what if you leave on the bike ride with the plan, but it's not rigid? You already know there is only a 30 percent chance (or less) that it will be the ride you expect and many other possibilities might play out (which is not a bad thing!). And then the chain breaks. You are *not* disappointed or frustrated, since you do not live in the illusion that you can control Life. You are open and might even be able to see the possibilities, beauty, or perfection of this moment. Maybe you decide to walk the bike and call a friend to chat. Maybe you walk and find a new coffee shop on the way. Or maybe you simply get tired while walking home and learn something from this experience.

Some of you might feel like giving up if life is so uncertain anyway? If you can't plan it all perfectly, what's the point? We have no power, you might think.

Well, as I mentioned earlier, just because you cannot predict it, it doesn't mean you do not have **power** or the ability to make a **choice.** It's just that this power of choice is not based on predicting by using the Calculator.

It is based on Truth and reality. You have an amazing system to guide you every single moment of the day: your heart, your feelings, and intuition. It's just a bit rusty due to years of being ignored!

And our willingness to do something that feels right without knowing or predicting the *exact* outcome might lead to something amazing and completely unknown and unimagined by us!

So, keep asking yourself:

"What do *I feel* I should do? What *feels right for me*?"

You might feel like taking an art class, even though you have no idea where that will go. You have never taken an art class, so how can you possibly base the decision on your past "known" information?

Maybe taking it will bring you peace, joy, or a new friend—who knows?!

So, if you feel like taking an art class, then do it! No questions asked. No hesitation. No second-guessing. It is the right path if it feels right to you.

When spontaneous action comes from within, it can sometimes feel like an eruption.

Go there!

And here's something super awesome... our Calculator head is now *serving us* instead of being our master! We first choose from the heart, from intuition, and then the Calculator head can help us *execute* our choice.

For example, using my heart and intuition, I might choose to build a treehouse, and my Calculator head can now help me get it going and do the calculating and measuring. Perfect!

Letting Go Can Be Love

As we start to move toward the unknown and follow ourselves, we might be faced with having to let go of many things. And it can be difficult. I had to let go of someone I love, at least for now. I had hopes and expectations that certain things would go a certain way, the way I wanted them to.

It didn't happen.

The day I let go of all this expectation, I felt a huge wave of unconditional love for the person instead of feeling like I was abandoning them.

It's interesting how letting go can be love, how distance can be love, and how "not helping" can be love. Many people think this is giving up, but maybe it's just trusting people and the universe.

The message is: I love you even if you don't deal with the issue. I won't be able to be close to you for now, but I love you!

To me, this feels very unconditional. *Conditional* love is the following: "I love you only if you fix yourself or act how I want you to."

So, letting go *while* still loving someone is an act of both forgiveness *and* pure love. You are not giving up on them; **you are letting life take care of them.**

You are not abandoning them. You are trusting them. You are not leaving them. You are there when they come to you in a healthy way.

We cannot rush another person on their path. This has been one of my hardest lessons. It's *their* responsibility, and their growth and healing has to be done in their own time.

If we do try to rush others to move at a faster pace than they're ready for, they might take this as demeaning—that we think *they can't do it on their own.* Or maybe it's just not the right time for them. Or maybe, it may be sad but necessary to allow people to suffer the consequences of their choices until they're able to see clearly. We can gently guide them, but sometimes we have to wait until **they are ready** to see how their choices matter and impact them, to see **their own power** to cause themselves harm or to heal themselves.

It can be difficult to feel other people's emotions, knowing we cannot do "their inner work" for them. But when others are suffering, we have a choice. We can choose to suffer with them— or we can choose *not to suffer* with them.

Instead, we can choose to be well and to be there for them as a supportive, strong, and flexible tree. We can help by listening, guiding (at times), and maintaining good energy ourselves.

As we become less controlling and stop taking responsibility for other people's emotions or lives, we don't experience the same rise in emotions when others have emotions.

We can allow them to experience their own emotions while remaining calm and easy, holding space for their Truth.

> "Wherever you stand, be the soul of that place." – Rumi

Harmony

ALL ACTIONS OF TRUTH AND LOVE are positive and have a major impact; all actions of dishonesty and control are not positive, and are weaker than the power of Truth and Love.

It's all about energy, but the universal direction is positive, and we are drawn to the positive. This is why you are drawn to read this and other similar books and to help yourself.

This is also why it's so important to align with your own Truth. If everyone does this, then everything will be at peace and in harmony, because each person is at peace and in harmony with themselves and with Life.

Moving Your Body

WITH A BIT OF COURAGE starting to rise, we can start to move the way we feel like without being controlled by the Calculator head or the outside world.

We can start to *be moved* by music, by our heart's desire, and by the universe. We can come back to life!

There is a difference between *choppy* movements and *fluid* movements. Choppy movements, controlled by the Calculator head, are more regimented and rigid than fluid movements. If you move rigidly, can you try to move freely without anticipation, plan, or judgment?

So many of us are afraid to move and show our bodies, and even to speak in public. But being ourselves includes feeling and moving in alignment with that true inner self. It takes Courage to go towards this way of living.

You can start by trying to exercise this freedom at home in the privacy of your own room. Notice what it feels like when you do. We need to *embody* all this energy, this sense of self, this freedom, and self-acceptance, not just think about it.

It's all about control vs. freedom.

Do you allow yourself to *be moved*? Or are you always controlling everything... even yourself? Exercise your freedom by releasing control and criticism and **moving the way your body wants.** Your body knows what to do. Trust it! The body always goes towards healing and joy.

The next time you hear a song you like, can you allow your feet to move freely out of your head's comfort zone, within your body's Truth zone?

And if you form a Courage Group with others to discuss the chapters in this book and invent exercises to encourage each other, try this practice:

First, each person makes a movement of any kind. Second, everyone can notice any judgment they might have about their *own* movements. Third, everyone can then note any judgment they have towards others. Judgment doesn't necessarily mean you are in full negative criticism mode. Judging whether you did something "right" or "wrong" is *not* freedom.

Discuss all this openly.

I feel I am able to watch someone walk and immediately sense whether they are rigid or fluid. I feel a person's gait is a **reflection of the level of the inner freedom they feel to be themselves.**

Can you give yourself permission to feel some freedom today by releasing control and just feeling your body and moving freely in your environment?

Fluidity with Gravity

ALL PRACTICES WHICH ALLOW US to feel the body will also help us feel gravity more fully, and this is no small thing! It is literally the way to **feel secure and supported**.

Gravity is a relationship that you were born with; it is your first relationship, one with your unconditionally loving and unabandoning Mother Earth. If you have trouble feeling this, then go outside, take your shoes off, and sit on the grass. Exhale to deepen your connection.

When we learn to feel our body and feel the ground, we start to feel more stable in any position, not only sitting.

If, however, your body is "frozen" in many spots, then you cannot move using all the possibilities that your body has available. Just imagine if you could only do one hundred movement combinations with your body: Do you think you would feel as safe and secure *gravity-wise* as the person who has a repertoire of endless fluid movement combinations? They are able to experience so many combinations to feel stable and in harmony with gravity!

This flexibility and fluidity are essential to our wellbeing.

Suppose you realize that parts of your body are frozen or rigid from being rejected so often or from any traumas you've experienced. In that case, many somatic practices will allow these body parts to move again. The *Feldenkrais Method* can be particularly helpful. It is a respectful and non-forceful method that can allow you to feel all the possibilities of movement, flexibility, and mobility. Many other movement and somatic practices also incorporate feeling, trust, and acceptance.

To "unstick" or "unfreeze" physical movement habits and re-
strictions, you can also try dancing *freely* or moving *freely*.

Feel your body fully and allow it to move as it needs. Stop
controlling and being controlled inside, and just move naturally!

If you're not used to such freedom, perhaps stand up with
music on and ask each part of your body what it feels like doing.
You can say, "Leg, move as you wish," "Chest, move as you wish,"
"Hips, move as you wish," and so on.

Moving naturally means moving *with* your nature, which is
part of the earth and the Universe.

Calm and Excitement

WHAT IS SO "GOOD" ABOUT always being calm?

A "calm" person can be passive-aggressive or demeaning with their facial expressions. They can be dismissive. Don't be fooled by an outward appearance of calm. It is not the same as being internally relaxed, kind, and at peace.

I've seen many instances where people want others to "calm down" when they are upset, crying, or even excited about something. This is controlling and doesn't allow for the range of human emotions, which are real, wise, and guide us.

Unless someone expresses their lack of calm by lashing out, disruptive behavior, or affects you in a way that you feel you need to set boundaries, **then why pressure someone to calm down so fast?** This leads us all to try to find a quick fix for any rise or discomfort. As a result, we turn to alcohol, excessive exercise, binge-eating, and other escapes, instead of looking at the disturbance, understanding it, and allowing it to process and pass fully in its own time. Forcing ourselves or others to calm down too quickly leads to anxiety, as we are not allowing the emotion to be fully felt so it can move through us.

Some people can alleviate their anxiety by allowing themselves to feel their core emotions, such as sadness, anger, fear, disgust, or excitement *in the body* and expressing them fully. When you find yourself feeling anxious, try to observe the body to see what *underlying emotion* is there, and allow it to surface without guilt or shame. You may need to take breaks when overwhelmed, of course, but then, can you come back to allowing your body to express itself?

Back to this obsession with "calm"—it can also affect our ability to be excited!

Excitement is awesome, but so often, we are told to repress it. There's nothing wrong with feeling calm, of course, but there is also nothing wrong with feeling excited!

Some people think that meditating is just sitting there. But once we sit there, face our pain, and know our center, sometimes it's **time to take action and not just be calm and passive in the face of what you need to do in this world.**

Feel what you feel passionate about or what drives you to act... and just start!

"Set your life on fire. Seek those who fan your flames." – Rumi

Practice Exercising Your Freedom

IT'S A FUNNY IDEA THAT we would need to "practice" using our innate freedom. Yet, I do think it takes some practice.

Practice today by going for a walk and making some silly move you feel like doing.

Maybe try humming in public or simply wearing what you feel like wearing. You can even spin around in a circle in the middle of the supermarket if you feel like it.

Freedom is actually scary for many people. "What will happen if I am *me*? If I start to show myself?"

Well, here's another question:

What will happen if you don't?

Exploring Beauty

BEAUTY IS EVERYWHERE. BUT IF you have an obsession with perfection, you cannot appreciate the beauty of asymmetry. You end up always trusting only instruments to measure things, instead of **trusting your senses and allowing your eyes, ears, hands, and heart to see and feel beauty.**

Can you choose where to hang art on the wall without using a measuring instrument and making everything "perfect" instead of beautiful?

Can you try to see beauty without measuring one thing against another? Can you see the essence of someone's humor, their softness, or their beauty *without comparing* it to what you perceive in another person? Can you just see their beautiful essence?

Trust all of your senses—sight, hearing, smell, taste and touch, and what you feel with your heart during every opportunity, as they are able to feel everything. They are here and available to you always.

May you access your peace and infinity now.

Being Sensitive

THIS IS SUCH A COMMON sentence: "You're being sensitive."

Yes, I am.
This is my strength.
I feel things.
I feel the world around me and inside of me.

For my whole life, I thought this was a weakness, because I didn't understand what was happening. If you're sensitive and a people pleaser, or if you're sensitive and governed by others' perception and their idea of whether you are lovable, worthy, or "good enough," then life is so very difficult! Maybe you read everyone's body language and can feel everything they feel and think and adjust yourself accordingly. This is how empaths can get *weakened*.

You might feel someone's simple negative tone or gesture like a tornado and adjust your behavior immediately.

But once we learn to assert ourselves and have boundaries, and once we do not need external approval, and once we distinguish our own feelings from *their* feelings and we don't try to *fix other people's feelings* or feel responsible for them, we become EMPOWERED.

And now, we can use our emotional intelligence and ability to feel everything—our ability to understand ourselves and others—to respond with wisdom and resolve as we follow our Truths.

When this happens, the EMPOWERED EMPATH will lead our world into a more peaceful existence.

Here's an example of how an Empowered Empath (which I believe most of us are capable of becoming) might function when they get a "feeling."

1. **Stop and Feel.** They stop and spend time figuring out *what* they feel. They are able to look within and figure out, "Oh, I'm mad."

2. **Curiosity and Self-Trust.** With their self-compassion, they do not criticize, second-guess, or invalidate themselves and their feelings, but rather wonder, "*Why* am I mad?" while trusting there must be an understandable reason.

3. **Self-Awareness and Clarity.** They spend time to calm down enough to understand why they have this feeling. Maybe they figure out it's because they felt someone was dismissive towards them, or trying to control them or someone they love.

4. **Stop and Think.** Because they understand through their empathy and emotional intelligence that this other person is not able or willing to see this right now, perhaps due to their own unresolved issues, and because they understand that the other person is a person worthy of respect, the Empowered Empath **stops again** before lashing out or personally attacking the other person with their anger, while still holding and trusting their anger and inner compass.

5. **The Power of Choice.** With so much information and clarity, they are able to make a choice about what to do about the situation, which was clearly not okay for them,

while staying in alignment with their feeling and inner compass. They don't blame. They know their power. They might choose to spend less time with a person, tell a friend who can understand, or perhaps speak directly to the person and share their view, while knowing they cannot control them.

6. **Outlet**. To let the rest of the energy out, they might cry, scream, practice a martial art, or go for a jog.

The pause (Step 4) between the anger and the action, while trusting their inner compass and while understanding the difficulty the other person must be in, represents intelligence. Therein lies the opportunity to use their **power of choice in the best way**.

Example 2:

1. Person A is mad and tells the Empowered Empath.
2. Assuming Person A is not yelling or otherwise abusive, the empath can listen and understand (also assuming they are not overwhelmed themselves, in which case they would set boundaries on their ability to listen at that moment). They do not try to fix the other person's feeling, knowing it's not their job and it's not *their* feeling. They can *hold space* for the other person's feelings.
3. The Empowered Empath can help guide the other person in making choices for themselves.

A compassionate person feeling, understanding, and empowering others while holding themselves in stability can lead our world in the "right" direction.

Listening to Others

How DO YOU LISTEN TO others? Are you judging or listening?

"How are you doing?" is a serious question to ask another person! The quality of their answer is dependent fully on the quality of your listening. If no one shares details with you whether at work or at home, for example if your kids do not tell you anything, it is likely a reflection of your ability to listen and your level of acceptance. This is worth looking into.

If you are lacking empathy, and are not easily able to understand where people are coming from, you are likely to have communication and relationship difficulties. You are likely having a lot of critical thoughts. Or you might think many things are about *you* instead of listening and understanding. You might be more inclined to take things personally. Empathy, and being compassionate, is something you can learn and practice, first with yourself and then with others.

All the people in your "circle" need and deserve listening and support, so please do not emotionally abandon or weaken them by criticizing, dismissing, and judging them. Do what you can to support them (within your limits and for the right reasons, of course).

Support might just mean:
- a kind word
- listening
- a caring touch
- believing in someone.

Try to avoid "taking over" someone's life or trying to constantly "rescue" them. This might be based on your own fears of abandonment or lack of self-worth. Doing so is counterproductive since it does not honor the path, wisdom, and pain that the other person might need to go through.

You can "let go" of a person and still be there for them.

Respecting Others

WE OFTEN WALK AROUND THE world feeling like we are "respon-sible" for others. Let's look at this for a moment.

We cannot make other people happy. Trying to control other people's emotions by "making them happy" is still control, and besides, we are human and not meant to be happy all the time anyway!

So, if every time you see another person is sad and your first thought is that you want to *make them happy*, you are not al-lowing them their process, their time, and adequate space for their feelings to exist.

Instead, you can validate, give them space to share, and allow them the time they need to cry or process their pain. This is more respectful. And then perhaps offer solicited advice, some words of hope or to do an activity that can bring a needed change of scenery.

Even in a situation when there is conflict, or the other per-son is frustrated about something, we can learn to listen well, understand their point of view, and empathize.

This can help us make wise decisions about what we want to do without being controlled or controlling.

Connection

ALTHOUGH THERE IS A TIME and place for solitude, we also know and feel at a deep level that we gravitate towards connection with others because our nature is togetherness. Our nature is to be connected to everyone and everything.

We are designed to connect **heart-to-heart,** not head-to-head. There is energy in the heart. We can feel this.

But until we truly connect with ourselves and with our own hearts, we cannot fully connect with others.

Unfortunately, many people are disconnected from their own hearts, especially since many societies reward the "thinking head" with credit, jobs, and approval. This is similar to living like robots, controlled from the outside and not really being here or present. We are completely disconnected from our paths and from the earth. When we just try to get things from each other, we cannot *connect* to each other as responsible, whole, and supportive beings.

But slowly, as you learn to live your own authentic life, you can come back to yourself and towards living from the inside out. You will slowly start to feel more connected with others on a different level!

No one has to give up power to connect.

As you become more open and honest, others around you will naturally start to open up as well. Your new *way of being* is powerful and will impact others, whether through your boundaries, conversations, or energy.

Learning to validate yourself and others will inspire even more opening! And you will start to allow yourself to be a bit more vulnerable and to trust those who know how to support you. This means, as we saw, not opening up to friends or therapists who are dismissive, controlling, or need to feel needed, powerful, and all-knowing.

And if you find that someone whom you are trying to relate to is closed despite your efforts, you might need to give them space; they are not ready.

It will get easier and easier to feel your way through this. Slowly, you will start to gravitate toward other open humans, and you'll encourage others simply by your openness.

The more of us who are open and honest,
the more we will all feel supported,
respected, and connected.

Uncontrollable
Power

Inner Power

INNER POWER COMES FROM INNER knowing—the knowing of our perfect loving nature and innate abilities which come from this Truth. And this cannot be controlled by the outside world, since it is an innate power.

Power is not a bad word. It's not about trying to *overpower* others. We are simply living in our power and using it in its natural direction. It's not at all the same as being "forceful."

In his book *Power vs. Force*, David Hawkins writes, "Power wins over force because force moves against something whereas **power doesn't move against anything**. Force has to constantly be fed energy. Power is total and complete in itself and requires nothing outside itself. It makes no demands; it has no needs." [1]

Although force can bring some momentary satisfaction by maintaining our illusion of control of Life, **the power of our loving nature** and our compassion can bring lasting inner joy and peace, and can truly help and empower others. This is true power and not a weakness, as some might imagine.

Do you want to live an empowered life or a life where everyone forces and tries to control others to do what they want?

If you have decided to live in Courage and have faith in your choices, you can start to live from the *inside*. It's a choice to move *away* from a life dictated by force and control and **towards a**

---

[1] Hawkins, David. *Power vs. Force*. Hay House, Inc.

life directed by innate power and love. It's a turning point that takes Courage.

Hopefully, this book allows you to feel the Courage I have had to muster throughout the years. **May it be contagious for you!**

Every choice made from a space of this kind of power becomes "good." This is never resigning or giving up.

Even resignation from a position (let's say on a Board of Directors) can be done with the choice not to be in any given organization anymore and to voice that refusal from a position of power.

Resigning is not resigning.

Complying is not complying.

Every move or choice can be powerful depending on the source and **intention of the action.**

And life is on your side and guiding you from within.

Always.

Whose Side Are You On?

IN THIS QUESTION LIES THE problem. Who said we should take sides? Why not take **everybody's side?**

By understanding yourself, you take responsibility to do your best to take care of yourself and your needs.

By understanding others, you give them information and a reflection of their Truth... and thus encourage them to move towards what they feel is best for them. There's no side.

By expressing your Truth and boundaries in any context you are not against anyone. You are for yourself, trust yourself and a set good example for others.

If they have not managed to see their Truth, speak their Truth, or heal from their pain, why would you be *against* them?

If they are trying to control you, then set your boundaries, speak your Truth, and do what you have to do *with resolve*, even if that includes distancing yourself or speaking out and being an activist. But why be "against" them?

Are you against a person who is clearly struggling with anxiety or feeling so unsafe or insecure in the world that they need to control everyone and everything?

Don't allow yourself to be controlled or put down! Leave their presence, do what you need to do, acknowledge your feelings, and get help. But at the end of the day, recognize the Truth—that someone else is struggling and this has nothing to do with you. This knowledge can help you take the right actions and prevent any possibility of hate.

Hate only exists in the ignorance of the Truth; in your inability to understand what is actually happening in yourself, and thus, in another.

Energy for Life

You might sometimes feel like you don't have energy... but it will come! Continue to be aware, process all your pain and hurt (alone or with help and support), and then just wait for internal clarity on what you are to do next.

If you accept all reality instead of sitting in avoidance or denial, and stop wasting energy by constantly comparing reality to your expectations, then life energy will come and flow naturally, and inspire you to do what you are to do. To act when you are to act. To sit when you are to sit.

Trust in this.

I've mentioned this before, but I'd like to say it again: On some days, you might only be able to get out of bed. That's fine. Just do what you can. Keep taking action and keep making choices. Otherwise, you'll always "let life happen to you." Action and choice are about living life fully, whatever the external circumstances.

If you avoid and delay life, you are like a bird in a cage, even though the door is wide open. You can fly into the unknown versus living in this "known" cage. Go towards the unpredictable!

Sitting in constant indecisiveness is sitting in the lack of choice, the lack of power. You merely think life will work itself out. This is not the "Trust in Life" I've been talking about.

To Trust Life, you must also **see you are a part of it**, so you do your part and stay connected.

Just keep acting from your center as you were designed to— guided by your inner compass versus outer governing.

This is your Personal Revolution!

Express Yourself

Every day is an opportunity to express yourself from the heart, not the head. If you don't express yourself naturally, you will have emotional stress.

In the heart, we have a flame which expands as we express our Truth and slowly uncover our purpose. Just express from the heart, and the words, the art, the movement, the tears—or whatever is natural—will come.

Life is energetic, not just physical. Robots will never be able to mimic this—at least not the part of life that emanates from the heart. Robots can only mimic life in the head.

We feel most alive when we quiet the processor and wake the heart—at any age, at any time, no matter what is happening.

Slowly get in tune with your inner child, with music, with everything! **You will begin to flow and move freely.** Listen to your heart, move your eyes and see, and feel, feel, feel everything. Sense, sense, sense everything—expand and merge.

Express yourself. Don't underestimate your life story. Maybe one conversation will change the world. These are the cards you've been dealt, and now...

Live your essence. Unapologetically.

Find out what touches your heart, for no matter what happened or happens, *no one can take that from you.* You can do this no matter what the external circumstances.

> "Let yourself be silently drawn by the strange pull of what you really love. It will not lead you astray." – Rumi

Life Purpose

WHAT IF I TOLD YOU your purpose in life is to be you and to trust that this is all you are *supposed* to do? This is precisely what I believe:

Your life purpose is simply to

be y♥u

and to

express yourself.

This will look differently for everyone. Your purpose will show itself naturally and effortlessly from within you once you are clear about your accountability and accepting of who you are.

There is no need to worry about nor to try hard to find your purpose. Stressing about life's purpose is like stressing about **being you.** Because you can't "find it." It's already there. You just need to remove the layers. (More easily said than done!)

So don't try to find your purpose. Find **Y♥U**... and the purpose will come to you.

Look for what is *effortless*. Effortless is not necessarily what you are "good at" though. You might be great in math but hate it.

Therefore, doing math can drain all your energy even though you're good at it.

On the other hand, you might struggle with playing an instrument and have no "talent," but in those moments, you *effortlessly* love to play the instrument, and you start to feel your ability to create sounds. In those moments, you are learning to create from within and building confidence. Effortlessly.

We are all "creative." We are all creators from within.

> "Everyone has been made for some particular work, and the desire for that work has been put in every heart." – Rumi

Ask for a Hand, Give a Hand

WE MIGHT NOT EVEN BE aware of our needs if they have been suppressed by others or ourselves. It is a long road to first see that you matter and then to uncover your needs.

But once we know we are valuable as we are, without "doing" anything—once we understand that we are a whole universe within, with a *duty to express our deepest self*—we can start to see our needs and feel a *duty* to take care of ourselves. We understand that we matter and belong to this world, and we want to be well so that we can carry out our life purpose of expressing ourself. This is not ego. This is true self-knowing, where one feels their innate value and belonging in the world.

We all have a basic need for support, even if we figure out our "purpose," or the next step on our path. It might not be an easy one. It might be very challenging. We may need people to support the process—to listen to us, to offer advice when we ask for it, and to hold space for us and our tears. This is not the same as them solving our issues, saving us, or "making us feel worthy."

We are human, and being human is hard. **A simple smile can lift a person, ignite a fire, and move mountains.** We need to support each other through our different paths. People want to help, so do not be afraid to ask for it.

Ask for a hand and give a hand.

It's that simple.

The Butterfly Effect

As described in an earlier chapter, the Butterfly Effect is the mathematical understanding that the sensitive dependence on initial conditions makes it so that a small change can result in large consequences later.

The term is associated with the work of mathematician and meteorologist Edward Norton Lorenz, who used the example of how a tornado can be influenced by a distant butterfly flapping its wings several weeks earlier.

Here are some examples of the Butterfly Effect:

The Police

At the time, it had been four months of difficulty for me, with the last two days being extremely challenging.

I managed to drive my daughter to school, although I was almost completely emotionally broken—and on the way home, the police stopped me for making an improper stop.

I was desperate to share my predicament with anyone, although my intention and purpose were not to get out of a ticket. Needing to be heard, I looked at the policewoman and told her, "I'm not trying to get out of the ticket and will respect your decision, but my family has been going through a very difficult time." I then spoke about a few things with which I was dealing, sobbing as I did so. The officer looked at me, gave me back my license, and said, "I am a mother too."

This act of compassion, this small light in a dark day, inspired me to start a journal to attempt to catch some light every day. This activity got me through some very dark times.

Who knows how the trajectory of my life changed from that moment...

Hot Milk

I got out of the car and walked into a gas station to get warm milk to calm my nerves.

A man was ahead of me, but he looked at me and smiled, and told me to go ahead of him. I thanked him and told him he made my day since it was a difficult time.

His eyes were kind, and he wished me luck.I was instantly calmer and understood the power of a smile.

Who knows how the trajectory of my life changed from that moment...

Jazz

I saw a jazz piano performance. The piano player was so open, sharing himself fully as he played. It was very inspiring. I sat there, and my cells opened and felt in harmony with my environment. I slept peacefully that night and woke up better able to face the next day.

Who knows how the trajectory of my life changed from then on...

Opera Music

I played opera in my house. After a few moments, I noticed that the birds outside were responding and singing. It is interesting to think about how they are impacted by the sound of the human voice and everything we do.

Who knows how the trajectory of their lives changed from there...

Everything is connected.

Everything matters.

Everything affects everything.

> "Never squish a butterfly, it might just change the world." – My daughter, age 12.

Powerful Feminine Energy

OUR INNATE POWERS ARE SOMETIMES described as masculine and feminine energies (this has nothing to do with gender). We all have these powers.

The infinite power in us—called the sacred feminine life force—is said by many to have been dormant within for centuries. But it is always whispering.

When we are ready, our heart opens, this power within us rises, and we embody the ancient wisdom of unconditional love, thus becoming a powerful light on all our surroundings.

We don't need to *learn* the sacred principle of unconditional love. It is already here, there and everywhere and when it's time, we feel it, live it, and defend it with all our might.

Once we embody this energy, we are compassionate, creative, and intuitive. We live in Truth and guidance comes from the heart.

It is time for the feminine energy to rise in all of us.

It is time.

As mothers and fathers, our compassionate feminine energy allows children to cry and to make mistakes, showing them that they are worthy of unconditional love. We respect them and teach them that they do not have to "fit in," for how else are they to respect and accept other people if they do not accept or respect themselves? We teach them that adults are not "above them" as beings; that we are all equal beings going through different experiences.

The feminine energy is in all of us. It is open, compassionate, fluid, creative and connected, but also as ferocious as the tides in the ocean. Using this power, we are ready to destroy falsehood and let go of the old and create a new reality every moment.

It is time for the feminine energy to rise in all of us.

It is time.

The Masculine Energy

INSIDE ALL OF US, WE have a powerful energy that complements our feminine energy. It is protective and stable.

The masculine energy helps us hold ourself together and protect our well-being. When things are difficult and chaotic, our masculine energy is our "structure"—our spine, our back. It is a strong and supportive energy, just as the spine supports the body. It helps us stay grounded, and act with logic and clarity.

The healthy masculine energy is not controlling or abusive. It is supportive, decisive, and logical.

We can access our masculine energy by talking to ourselves in the following way:

"You can do this."
"You will be okay. I'm holding you."
"It's time to get organized and act."

Now *feel* and visualize your strength and stability in your spine, like a sword. Feel your back enveloping you and providing protection, stability, and structure. Feel the ground. I have used this internal visualization many times to hold myself together when I felt I was falling apart or to give me added strength, focus, and direction when I needed it while moving forward with an action I felt I must take.

Go and find your masculine energy inside when you need it. It's always there.

Wild and Free

MANY OF US HAVE HAD our wild and free nature, our pleasure, and our movements controlled.

Wildness and pleasure *are allowed* in dancing, in our sexuality, and in our voice.

Do not be afraid of your own wild side. Enjoy it!

Dance until you shatter yourself – Rumi

Belonging

IMAGINE THAT ALL YOUR DECISIONS come from inside, that you trust them, and that you even *trust your suffering* to guide you to the next move. That, whatever comes, you know you are armed with your inner compass.

You live in self-love, gravity, Truth, and according to your inner compass. There's not much left to worry about!

Without second-guessing, criticizing yourself, and worrying about the future and outcome, there's no anxiety.

As a sovereign being, you identify yourself as an individual—a unique human being who **belongs on this earth**.

You do not need anyone's
permission to belong.

Constantly Forgiving

WE ARE EASILY ABLE TO forgive as soon as we know the Truth, the whole story of a human experience.

So, for example, if we sat with a mother for one day, one year, or five years listening to why she gave up a child for adoption, we might *understand* why she made that choice. (Understanding has nothing to do with agreeing or excusing.) If we actually sat and listened, we could *understand* why someone spends so much time at the hairdresser. Why someone uses drugs. Why someone is unable to express their feelings, and so on. If we spent time, **we could understand what the other person's world feels like to them.**

But what if we don't know or have time to listen to their whole life story? Can't we understand and forgive without knowing their whole story? Can't we assume that they *must have some reason* for doing this, even one that we don't necessarily agree with?

Once we *understand ourselves* and know how to separate the person from the behavior, we no longer attack anyone deeply, since we understand that we are made of the same fabric.

Many people may not have processed their pain and matured emotionally in all ways. We can look at each person with compassion and understand that **they are still maturing emotionally, as we all are.** Perhaps they are lashing out or still learning to allow their emotions and how to trust themselves. Maybe they have unresolved traumas we don't know about.

This doesn't mean allowing "bad" behavior and not setting boundaries. Instead, it's about understanding and knowing that everything is forgivable! And everything is healable.

When you walk around the world with this energy, people **open up** with you. They feel you are not against them personally.

You now hold the power to open others up without doing anything at all!

Just by being you.

Constantly Learning and Growing

WITH OUR CURIOSITY CONSTANTLY WORKING and our criticism and self-doubt diminished, we have space for wonder and learning about whatever we are interested in.

Everywhere you go, everything you experience is an opportunity for opening and growth.

So, if you go for a walk, you are not wasting your energy thinking about what is good or bad, or what you can get from the outside world.

In that space, you might be able to see how a child is playing in the park, smile and get inspired to move in more flexible ways as you used to as a child.

You might notice an older person walking with a cane and remember not to give up.

If you speak to someone, instead of criticizing them, you might look for what is interesting in their thoughts and experiences.

You might start to learn a new instrument, read books, or simply sit with yourself.

You are able to learn and grow in any direction that feels right, following your own curiosity.

Your Body, Your Soul, and Gravity

How you view yourself affects how you view and treat your body. If you see your inner self as bad, it makes sense that you might self-harm, especially with all the punishing modeling you might have seen and felt from others.

If you see your inner self as a beautiful soul, a sweet essence in a body that is experiencing this thing called Life, **then the body is there to carry out your purpose.** Thus, you literally see your body as your temple.

There is a difference between taking care of your body for vanity, people-pleasing, or external validation (e.g., "I'm going to take care of myself so people like me and think I'm great and look good") and taking care of your body because it is the house of your spirit, essence, and soul!

In this way, the body is *literally* a temple. It is the house of you as a "divine" being.

So, don't worry about your body. Instead, look inside at your *true self.* Love yourself, and taking care of your body will naturally follow! Your body is a conduit for your soul work, or purpose. It speaks. Listen to it!

Many people who lead organized religions might view some of my words as sacrilege—especially my writing that we are all "divine," that we all have innate superpowers and wisdom, and that we are an extension of the universe and its beauty.

They are all entitled to their opinions.

As I listen to my *true self* and my body, I can feel everything. Starting with my feet, I can feel the ground, feeling safe,

241

and balanced. My ankles are flexible. My hips have power. My heart is open and my spine is strong and flexible. My eyes are open to seeing anything and everything, and to cry as I might need. My ears are listening to the sounds of the Universe. My hands can feel and touch from the heart, and I am open like a lotus for "direction" from above.

We can move our bodies more freely, with less rigidity and control once we have opened. It reflects our inner freedom. We feel as though our environment, our body, and our repertoire of movements is immense, having unstuck all the frozen parts.

When we are able to feel the repertoire of movement, we have choices, options, and fluidity to feel and react to our environment from a place of security.

This flexibility in interacting with gravity is no small thing! We feel more supported and stable, and we act from security. We feel our relationship with earth, with gravity, all the time.

We start to naturally move **from our being**.

We realize that we are a moving energy system, a living planet... always moving, always breathing.

Connectedness

As you become used to feeling the ground and your surroundings, you will come to see that gravity is not just from you to Mother Earth. You will constantly "gravitate" towards certain things and people and away from others, following your inner compass.

Like planets, we move and gravitate towards and away from. This is not because anything is bad; it's because you are better able to feel your way through life, and your comfortable nature allows others to gravitate towards you because of your way of being.

You have an energy that is accepting and non-controlling— first of yourself, then with life itself, and now with others.

And this type of respectful connecting is the cure to loneliness: It's when we realize that in fact, in an open state, **we are all connected and not alone at all.**

This feels like a true connection *to all* instead of a desperate and superficial attachment to a few. We are all one when we live and connect from the heart.

What A Powerful Human Being Looks And Feels Like

Freedom

Imagine...

Walking around life being you.
Not caring what others think about you.
Not needing anyone's approval.
Accepting all your feelings, passions, and interests.
Not feeling like you need to perform.
Not needing to shop, drink, or medicate to feel better.

It's possible.
Just remember who you are... a free spirit.
The rest will follow.

True Voice

IF YOU EVER TOOK A voice or singing class, you might see that many of the things we discussed here apply to your voice.

Take a breath, letting go of your jaw. Do not force the sounds but simply **allow them to emanate from the heart and body.** There is no force from the throat or from anywhere!

This is how you can sing or speak your Truth now. With no use of force, but from the *power within*. And the echoes and vibrations of the sounds will emanate from the crown of your head.

This voice of yours "sounds true," and others who are opening will feel it.

It has **power** without force.

Energy

WE NOW HAVE ENERGY BECAUSE we are following ourselves. We are not wasting energy on fitting in, pleasing, trying to get people to like us, overthinking, or having self-doubt. We are not wasting energy on blaming, controlling, manipulating others, or trying to control life. All of it takes up *so much* energy.

Our body has more flexibility and movement, is less controlled, and uses less energy to "stack itself" in its relationship with gravity.

Like a tree, we are rooted and flexible.

We are not seeking to be liked; we are not seeking happiness. We are just living as we are, including living all the challenges that will continue to come.

Our energy is now freed up. We can feel sadness and joy. We are living with power, and it takes no energy!

Effortless living. No forcing of yourself or others, just living your Truth and having the whole universe behind you. You are free to be and act as you see in every situation that arises.

And there is stability. Because YOU, connected to Life, are the constant in every moment and every situation.

Confidence

You NOW LIVE IN CONFIDENCE, not ego. You live in the confidence of knowing and feeling your essence, embracing it, and courageously living it. You also understand that others have their own essence (although it may be hidden under layers of untruths they have "learned").

This confidence cannot crumble under pressure **because it has the support of Truth and the Universe.** It is not *your* confidence. It's confidence in *life itself* that you embody.

Confidence is living without constant self-doubt, without overthinking, and without insecurity. Trusting that *you're supposed to be you...* and acting and expressing yourself accordingly.

You No Longer Hide

You NOW HAVE AN INFLATED heart instead of an *inflated ego*, and you are untouchable, since no one can touch that feeling. They can do anything to your body, but your sense of inner self is untouchable, unhurtable, stable, and clear.

People who are still doing controlling behaviors will keep doing what they do, *but they cannot control you inside and cannot hurt you deeply inside.* You remain intact and powerful. You are able to stay in your center and your Truth without attacking or demeaning anyone, and stay in loving understanding of others, even when disagreeing with them. This is **non-violent living and activism**.

This book is ultimately about a non-violent but highly powerful movement. A movement in which you are an *active* participant simply by *being you* and encouraging others to do the same.

A movement that is innately more powerful than control and has the backing of the Truth of the Universe. That is the "authority."

A movement which I am hoping you will join.

We need a **climate change**—a change of the climate within which most of us deal with one another. One where each person is very soft and strong at the same time. One where we are in balance.

This is the climate we need. The climate the world needs.

Soft and Strong

OUR INNER MASCULINE AND INNER feminine are now in balance and fluid. Both are available to be accessed when the right time calls for them.

An emotion rises, and our feminine energy is aware, open, powerful, compassionate, and accepting. Our masculine energy is also powerful and ready to act and support. And when we interact with another person, energy can be brought forth depending on what the situation requires.

In this balance, in being in touch with both parts of us, the masculine warrior-like protectiveness and the feminine power of unconditional love are ready to be of service.

We are soft and strong at the same time.

We are in balance.

Clarity

WHEN ALL OF YOUR ACTIONS come from knowledge of your right path, not self-aggrandizement or insecurity, those actions are infused with potent universal power and energy.

And it's not the actual actions that matter, but the intent from which they arise.

Being for yourself, in the deep sense, means you are for everyone.

You need to *feel this* to understand. Just keep living with compassion for yourself. The rest will follow naturally. Choices become effortless.

Everything will become as clear as the air on a winter day.

Inspiration and Vision

IN FRENCH, THE WORD INHALE is *inspire*. With every inhale, you breathe and are inspired.

Inspiration is constant now.

You are inspired to do things because they feel right even if they are hard. You feel alive and aligned.

You keep following this inspiration and intuition, which ignites a spark in your heart. An open heart is the answer to the elusive questions.

In every moment, you make choices based on inner clarity without questioning it. Then, you trust, and let life unfold. You are no longer constantly calculating and measuring. Without measuring and calculating, there is no ego.

You follow joy and what feels right, and measuring or analyzing doesn't matter. You follow your hunches and understand that your path might not be straight.

Your eyes and vision slowly become clearer. Instead of being "laser-focused" and having goals based on insecurity, you have a wider vision.

You are clear-voyant.

Fluidity

ONCE YOU FEEL YOUR WAY through life in this new way for some time, life starts to feel more stable. Yes, there will sometimes be sadness and even anger, but you are listening to yourself and taking action each time.

You are not stuck on things having to be a certain way, and you are learning to accept and be part of life. You make choices using your intuition and trust the outcome, even if it is not immediately apparent.

You no longer try to change people and life under the guise of love. You love without controlling because you have flexibility, trust in yourself and life, and know how to make choices.

Acting in accordance with intuition is fluid, self-assured, grounded, and non-violent, since it comes from clarity of self and not *against*-ness. You are not doing things against something or someone; you are not trying to force or control anyone. **You are just acting from your inner wisdom and your expanded and connected self.** Internally you are *for* everything and everyone.

Not only do you understand that you cannot control everyone and everything, but you also don't even *want to* control anymore. You are just living your own destiny, and everything is aligned: Your feminine and masculine side, your understanding of your deep good nature, and your clarity about the flow of life not being yours to question but yours to trust.

It takes no energy to act in accordance with intuition. No thinking, second-guessing, criticizing, or self-sabotage.

Your mind is free because your decisions and actions are fluid, as natural as an animal walking towards a stream to drink water.

Every experience is just an opportunity for you to make choices. That's your power—the power of being fluid and open to possibilities and feeling what you are to do every moment.

This is what "going with the flow" means!

We cannot force life to move a certain way. We must accept the reality of now. When we do this, we make choices instead of getting stuck by refusing to see or accept reality and Truth! This is how I understand Bruce Lee's expression, "Be like water."

We understand that wanting things to happen a certain way removes our power—our power of being fluid in the moment and to make choices. Trying to control yourself, others, and life is a useless mission. Expecting things to go a certain way is futile.

You can make choices every moment... and that's more than awesome!

You are one player empowered by life, energy, and fire. When you make a move, **you move the whole world**, for the whole world is moved by every movement.

If you want peace, then just sit in your power and move from your nature.

This is inner peace.

Love of Life

I KNOW I AM NOT JUST me. I am fed energy, I am the universe, and I am an expression of all. (As we all are.)

We all have inner guidance, inner power, inner life force, an inner compass, and an innate ability to forgive, love, feel, listen, see, and cry. Everything else comes from there.

My ability to see me is the ability to see and feel all, because all is expressed everywhere.

And I can see how life is beautiful with all its waves, as it moves with the flow of positive energy. I can experience moments of natural ecstasy by just listening or moving to music.

An ocean has tornadoes, hurricanes, and storms, and it is still perfect and beautiful in its entirety—and so is life.

In the words of Victor Frankel:

"Say Yes to Life.
In Spite of Everything."

Compassion

THERE IS A SAYING THAT goes, "When we are walking around with a bleeding heart, compassion is what dries it."

Showing compassion for someone at the right time—understanding their struggle or pain—is so powerful. Once you use this power on yourself, you can offer it to others.

What can be more powerful than allowing someone the space to shed some healthy tears? It's like being a superhero! But you can only do it correctly once you have done it for yourself and have no agenda to get something from the other person.

Your softness is stable and strong.

It's always possible to understand others.

Not agree with, not excuse certain behavior, but to simply understand someone.

This is the highest form of intelligence that, unfortunately, is not taught in schools or many homes... yet.

Inner Peace

ONCE WE UNDERSTAND THE WHOLE truth of why we are hurt and what we need, once we take responsibility to heal our own wounds, save our own life, and set all necessary boundaries, *only then* are we at a place where we can also look at the situation from the other point of view and understand there is innocence in all humanity.

How can we not love the innocent?

Actions can flow naturally from this place. Not from wanting or needing anything from another person, a tree, or an animal, but from having so much clarity, power, and understanding that one is full and has something to offer the tree, the person, and the animal.

Inner peace does not mean doing nothing. It means **you are at peace with what you are doing.**

And only when someone is *in peace,* can it be said that their actions are *peaceful,* whether those actions are to teach, interact with children, be a veterinarian, or protest against injustices.

All actions become healthy and *right.*

Contagious

In each heart, there is a potential for fire waiting to be ignited. And the fire in our *own* hearts can be the spark that ignites that of another.

One simple act of compassion, such as smiling at someone, can be the spark, that inspires them to consider their value and nature.

This is contagious and can spread like wildfire. In this way, our heart is like the sun—an ever-burning fire.

Do Not Leave Anyone Behind... In Heart

EVERY MOVE YOU MAKE CAN change the world. A nudge in the right direction, or a kind word at the right time and place, can change everything.

We can do this by being a mirror... a clear mirror, just reflecting Truth. And by looking in the mirror, a person can see more clearly... and choose if they want to change direction.

It's effortless.

If someone is moving in what appears to be an unhealthy direction, it is hard to stop them or force them to redirect. If you just kindly reflect their Truth by being a clear mirror, and also share your Truth with love, they might "see." And even if they don't right away, they may remember what you showed them and might change direction themselves when they are ready.

Hold people in your heart—it has so much space! And no one around you will feel alone or abandoned.

> "The universe is my country, and the human family is my tribe." – Khalil Gibran

Merging into the Environment

THINK OF YOURSELF AS HAVING inward and outward tentacles that can touch and tune into everything that is happening at the same time. Think of yourself as being in tune with your feelings, inner childlike innocence, your vibrations, breath, and heartbeat, and everything within you, and *at the same time*, being in tune with the outside environment, all the way into space. You are able to *tune in* to your inner and outer world because you are not living in your head.

With this openness to receive information **from anywhere and everywhere** and your head not blocking information with its resistance or refusal to see anything, you can see and feel everything, listen to your heart, and move freely.

When we sense everything and our heart is so wide open, we can experience moments when our being feels so expanded that we can feel life beyond our "individual self."

We have merged with our environment, with the Universe, and are immersed in perfection in motion.

This is peace in Truth.

You cannot *choose* to do this. I believe this is a *natural state* that can occur anytime, to anyone, when the time is right. I have had glimpses of this, and I know it is possible and true.

So, put some music on and sing or dance. Surround yourself with free humans. You know what this feels like. You have felt glimpses of this freedom and ecstasy in simply being many times, especially when you were younger.

Remember and go there!

Unconditional Love

Rᴇɢᴀʀᴅʟᴇꜱꜱ ᴏꜰ ᴀɴʏ ꜱɪᴛᴜᴀᴛɪᴏɴ, ʙᴇʜᴀᴠɪᴏʀ, choice, and cir-
cumstance, there is the potential for unconditional love, of living with an inflated heart instead of an inflated ego. Once you
have accepted everything and let go of control, this energy—this
powerful energy that we all possess—is the natural extension.

Once you have passed the stage of "loving" for your own purpose of feeling worthy, once you have set all boundaries, once
you are Y♥U, and once all is in place, there is pure love that can
be transmitted **beyond our current understanding**.

Unconditional love is beyond time and space. Even if you
can't *do* or *get* anything, you can still love. You do not need
someone's permission to love them. You can do so even from a
distance and it can be felt, since our heartstrings are connected
once we have interacted with someone.

It is interesting how giving up control leads to so much power.
True love has no conditions and does not require anything. Not
even being on the same side of the world.

True love is like a river. It will find a way around every possible hindrance to keep flowing freely.

This is our ultimate superpower.

> "There is a window from one heart to
> another heart." - Rumi.

My wish for you...

Every experience, trauma, pain, beautiful moment, and teacher brought me to write this book. And everything you have lived has brought you here. And here we are together.

I hope the seeds have been planted in you to see and feel your Truth and potential—not to achieve, but to be who you truly are. That will tell you what you should be doing here.

You are a flower. Beautifully, effortlessly alive. For it is effortless to do things aligned with *you*. And when all is said and done— if you are true to your essence and live it, I believe you will naturally, by no force or effort, be compelled to help your brothers, sisters, your immediate neighbours, all distant fellow humans.

You are now in a position where you can *feel* the essence of other human beings, regardless of any of their behaviors, words, or thoughts. And you don't have to *do* anything, as simply being yourself in their presence is **already a powerful transformer!** They can feel that you see them and their goodness, and this observing has an impact on their "spin" or wavelike properties (as in quantum physics). It *moves* things.

You can also encourage others in whatever way comes naturally by the fact you trust their innate wisdom, trust life, and believe in them. This can trigger a **virtuous circle**. All this with no effort, because all you have to do is **be Y♥U**—and this is contagious. I wish you luck in your quest and believe you can do it.

With love, *Sandy* ♥

About the Author

Sandy Stream is an author and activist whose work stems from the belief that everyone deserves and is capable of finding peace and warrior-like strength within themselves. After teaching law for 20 years, raising her two children, and facing a life full of adversities and lessons, she decided to turn her efforts towards facilitating workshops to encourage others to live in peace and power.

thecouragecircle.com